THE RATIO OF SUCCESS

ZED AYESH

THE RATIO OF SUCCESS

A blueprint for achieving your goals

ZED AYESH

PASSIONPRENEUR® PUBLISHING

Publishing information
Publishing and design facilitated by Passionpreneur Publishing
A division of Passionpreneur Organization Pty Ltd
ABN: 48640637529

Melbourne, VIC | Australia
www.passionpreneurpublishing.com

This book is dedicated to my father –
a man of courage and arduous work –
and to my wife and kids,
whom I am lucky enough to regard as my best friends.

TABLE OF CONTENTS

INTRODUCTION

For more than thirty years, I have studied a lifestyle strategy known throughout my life circle as The Ratio of Success. This strategy is not a mathematical formula, but a formula built on simple principles of no-nonsense wisdom that have proven crucial to my success in both my business and personal lives. The Ratio of Success continues to be the guide and measure I use to ensure I achieve my goals with facts that supports my continued achievements. In this book, I explain The Ratio of Success and how the application of these simple principles will help you achieve your goals and objectives and how you can attain the success you dream and hope for.

This book is not a manual full of tricks and gimmicks but requires you to recognise the single most valued resource in your possession and, more importantly, what you can do with that resource. The Ratio of Success is not a magical formula; reading this book alone will not do anything to change your life. However, applying this strategy in your life with consistent discipline and dedication will set your path toward a rewarding life, providing you with a sense of achievement that will impact all your future endeavours.

Most people today believe they know where they are going, but many are unsure of how to get there. It's easy to set our eyes on the prize ahead yet lose sight of the work required to navigate the obstacles, challenges, and options that are presented to us every moment of the day. There is no mobile phone app to map your life's path for you, so it is easy to simply overlook the need to strategically set and monitor the many goals necessary to get where you want to go. The beauty of The Ratio of Success concept is that you will begin seeing results immediately. Studies show that keeping records of your daily tasks will positively impact your day-to-day life, resulting in improved productivity and overall achievements.

My life's journey has not been easy. I did not come from a wealthy family and was fortunate to secure a scholarship to complete my university studies. Some would say I grew up in poverty – money was a luxury for my family – yet the values I gained working while others played during school holidays laid a lifestyle foundation that I continue to build on to this day. From an early age, I learnt success isn't about how much money you have in the bank or the type of car you drive. I've seen success in my life but that's not to say I am now wealthy. I started with nothing, and have made and lost millions of dollars, repeatedly, during my life. But it is these times that have taught me some of the hard lessons that I hope to impart to you in this book, lessons that I know will help you succeed.

On these pages, you will find all you need to know about discovering your Ratio of Success. How to develop it and apply it to every aspect of your life. From there, the world is yours if you choose to follow the lessons gained from experience.

I am honoured to guide you to the next level in your life, work, and business.

Zed Ayesh

CHAPTER 1

WHAT IS LIFE MADE OF?

It is an important question, but the more important question is: 'What is a good life made of?'

To understand the answer to this question, we first must know, in basic terms, what life is made of, regardless of whether it's good or not, normal, boring, dull, successful, or brilliant. By no means is this a deeply philosophical book, but it is a book with a simple idea about creating a successful, enjoyable, and meaningful life for yourself.

"Success is not a random act. It arises out of a predictable and powerful set of circumstances and opportunities."

— Malcolm Gladwell

Life is not a random act; it involves a series of circumstances controlled by our actions. In its simplest form, life is time.

But what is time, and what is it made of? I have spent years contemplating the value and meaning of time, single moments that, when combined, become hours, just as hours become days, days become weeks, weeks become months, and months become years.

We can't change the moments in history, but we can control the moments of today and tomorrow. So, my questions to you are: 'What type of life are you living now?' and 'What type of life do you want to live?' Bringing change to your life is the result of what you do in this moment of time, and the next, and the next.

This book is designed to challenge your consideration of time and identify the quality of life you want to live, the goals you want to achieve, and how you can successfully accomplish all that you want in life.

What you do in each moment of your life will decide the quality of your life. The sum of those moments is the sum of your life – it is as simple as that. This means that life achievement is effort management. What you do in each moment counts towards the quality of the sum of those moments. Remember, moments become hours, hours become days, and days become years.

What you do during these moments is the most important part of life. What you do and do not do will be the accomplishment of your life. Where you are today is the result of all the moments of your past. What you do with your moments today will determine where you are tomorrow. Our lives are indeed measured by time passing. For some, this just equates to age, but life is what we do within that time. Quality of life is the result of the quality of effort applied within time.

We think we are using, spending, or managing time, but none of these concepts is truly correct. We do not own time, nor do we have control over time.

How can we spend or use time if we do not own it or control it? Time cannot be captured, nor can it be controlled. It cannot be reproduced or recreated. The only thing we can control is our effort in that time; that is to say, what we 'do-in-time' paves the way to our destination.

It is safe to assume that we look at time as something we control through time-management tools, but do we? Are we not trying to feel good about ourselves by being busy and having many things to do? How often do we get distracted during the day? How often do we put off urgent things? How many times a day do we view, post, and endlessly scroll on social media? We are robbing ourselves of moments that will never be again, will never be recreated, and are gone forever, and we grow busier than ever with nothing to show for it. We ignore what counts, which is the quality of what we do-in-time. The type of effort and the quality of our efforts in those moments determine the output of our life.

We should not measure our lives by the amount of time passing, but by what we do-in-time.

As mentioned in Malcolm Gladwell's *Outliers*, to become an expert in a subject, you need to dedicate 10,000 hours of studying, practising, and working on that subject. If you think about it, 10,000 hours is about two hours a day, five days a week for twenty years, or four hours a day, five days a week for ten years. It could also be eight hours a day, five days a week for a little more than five years. If you are prepared to dedicate this time to a subject, then you are likely to become an expert or a specialist in that subject.

To compete in the Olympic Games, athletes practise for years. They practise every day, every week, and every month for years to be the best of the best. Elite athletes spend their waking moments practising and working towards achieving their goal of becoming gold medallists. Every single day, champions are made through dedication. Being a champion, like being successful, is not an accident or a stroke of luck even if some degree of talent is involved. It is the process of applying quality effort to a given moment and repeating that effort the following moment, and so forth, for as long as needed to become an expert at what you do.

Age is time passed – life is what you do in that time

In the pages to follow, I will share with you a few simple techniques that, if properly applied to your life, will guide you to success, to becoming a winner in life, to being what you want to be, to achieving your goals while living a fulfilling life in which every single moment counts.

First: 'Knowing yourself is the beginning of all wisdom.' - Aristotle

For thousands of years, elite individuals have discovered that without knowing yourself, you cannot succeed or live up to your potential.

Knowing yourself – i.e., self-discovery – is where all great achievements begin. Without knowing yourself, how would you act? You would act without understanding what you can and cannot do, what you like or dislike, what makes you happy or sad, what motivates or frustrates you, and how you are influenced by your surroundings. Psychological science shows us repeatedly that self-awareness is rarely comprehensive. Each of us seems to possess a great capacity for self-deception. Knowing yourself is where it all starts and ends. Extensive research shows that, as humans, we believe that we know ourselves. Yet, this is far from the truth; our thoughts and beliefs about who we are often are not true. We have a hidden mechanism inside us, known as self-deception. We hate pain. We do not like to be hurt by confronting ourselves. Therefore, our inner self creates self-deception to avoid pain and suffering, leading us to make excuses and stay in our comfort zone. Knowing yourself is where a good life starts and/or ends.

Second: monitor

You do not need research or complicated methods for self-discovery. This book is about much simpler, doable, tried and tested ways of getting to know yourself. It is self-discovery by monitoring your actions. This can be done by simply recording your daily activities for a period of six to eight weeks, noting the time taken for each activity without leaving any activity out – that includes sleeping, working, and commuting, and any other actions such as responding to emergencies or unexpected events.

I am willing to bet you money that what you believe about yourself is not one hundred per cent true. This bet is not to offend you but, rather, to show you that more than sixty per cent of people are not accurate in their self-assessments, particularly when it comes to how they spend their time. I've seen this repeatedly as the people I have coached, mentored, or led have looked at accurate records of their time and efforts and had the colour drain from their faces. This, while often shocking, is a profound starting point for change.

Psychologists have identified several ways of fooling ourselves: biased information-gathering, biased reasoning, and biased recollections. In his 2011 book, *The Folly of Fools: The Logic of Deceit and Self-Deception in Human Life*, Robert Trivers floated a novel explanation for such self-serving biases: we dupe ourselves to deceive others, and in doing so, create social advantage.

Monitoring your actions by recording them with accuracy and honesty in a journal or diary with the time logged for each action will have an immediate impact on your life. Just realising how things transpire daily is enough to alter your routines. Recording your daily actions is the only true way to self-realisation and self-discovery. All the other ways, without written proof, are self-deception. To know your true self is to record your actions and the time it takes to complete these actions. This becomes an eye-opening and life-changing exercise. In this book, I will give you powerful and practical strategies to transform the way you perform honest self-reflection and parlay this into action.

Third: discovery

Our perception of reality is not reality, at least not in its full extension. Moving from not knowing, from not understanding, to a full comprehension of reality is an 'a-ha!' moment of self-discovery. The results from examining our activities and time consumed are a reality check and confirmation that without knowing what is true and what is not, you cannot move forward. The self-monitoring exercise is the starting point; self-discovery forms the boundaries and the framework for the successful journey. The surprising news is that most of us, if not all, do not believe what we see with our own eyes. We do not believe the results of the monitoring exercise. We believe what is in our minds. We deceive ourselves day in and day out because it makes us feel good.

Following the monitoring exercise, we will discover the habits that drive us every day without consciously thinking about them. We will discover what we do versus what we think we do. And this will provide a better understanding of whether we are working towards our goals or not. For sure, this will be like a movie where we each become the star without knowing what the movie is all about. Self-discovery makes sure that we are not only the star of our life movie but also the director of that movie.

We believe we are effectively using our time. We believe that we manage our time and are in control, that we know what is going on, and that we are going in the right direction by doing what we do every day. Self-discovery will prove otherwise. It will prove that our self-perception is far from the truth.

The truth is that we are slaves to our habits. We will do anything to avoid pain, including the pain that comes from facing the truth. But to face the truth is to arm yourself with the greatest weapon you will ever have when it comes to achieving the life or success you want. I hope that in reading this book, you do so to transform into the best version of yourself.

Fourth: what is your ratio?

The beauty of time is that it cannot be reproduced, it cannot be captured, and it cannot be withheld. Once it's gone, it is gone forever; the clock keeps on ticking. Our time is indeed our life. But is that what you should be thinking? 'Am I growing older or is my life getting shorter?' Time has two dimensions when it comes to your life. The first is that we all share time in equal measure – we all have twenty-four hours a day. The second is that each one of us is limited to how many weeks we live, and this varies from person to person. This means that we exist on a reduced time scale with the passing of every moment. Our lives are getting shorter by the minute. How you spend your time is the most important part of life and is what makes the difference in the quality of life. And because no one can control time, what we do-in-time forms the difference and becomes the maker of success.

Fifth: results first

Life without goals is a wasted life. To get to where you are going, it's necessary to know where you are going first, with the destination in view. Working backwards from the intended result is the most effective way to achieve that result; it guarantees efficiency and eliminates waste and distraction.

In his book, *The 7 Habits of Highly Effective People*, Stephen Covey lists starting with the end in mind as the second most important habit. I couldn't agree more on that point. Major life achievements are not accidents; they do not happen by coincidence. Plans might change and require adjustment, as the road we start on might take us on detours from where we want to go. But without a plan, there will be no need for adjustments, and without starting the journey, we would never get anywhere. Starting from the end will help us to plan by choosing the right activities and by allocating sufficient time for such activities to reach our desired results.

Sixth: let's get unbusy

So much to do, so much going on, and so many opportunities – time-sucking activities are always at our fingertips. The world is changing, but time remains a constant; we still have 168 hours each week. Self-discovery that leads to knowing what consumes your time is the only way to differentiate yourself from others, and the only way to achieve success. With time being sucked away from us every moment, what not to do becomes far more significant than what to do.

Saying no to activities that waste time and being more selective in what we do-in-time is what counts in achieving a high-quality life. In today's fast-paced life, the choice of what we do-in-time forms the deciding factor between success and failure. The root of time-wasting habits is self-deception.

Seventh: design your pathway

At this point, you should know what you do-in-time. You have determined your goals, you have a vision of desired results you want to achieve, you have the desire and will to succeed, and you are ready to get going. But is that enough to be successful? We are never fully prepared for such a journey. It's not enough to decide on the goal to get it done. It's not enough to have a vision of the desired results – desire and will are not enough. What is needed at this stage is a process for how you are going to achieve your goals.

This is where planning becomes the next step of action, where planning becomes everything. It is easy to be distracted by the everyday hustle, demands, and responsibilities of life. We can no longer control our destiny without controlling a minimum amount of time and the activities within that time. Monitoring, self-discovery, and getting unbusy while starting with results first are all the tools you need for a successful life. Your time-ratio planning, if done correctly, is the canvas for success.

Eighth: big results, small projects

Big goals are not big projects; they are many smaller projects that lead to big results. Big goals can be overwhelming even without the distractions, demands, negative environments, unproductive habits, and change resistance that can easily derail any project. The planning to achieve results requires doing certain activities for different lengths of time repeatedly. Doing these activities will bring you closer to your desired goals. These activities must be broken down into smaller, individual tasks. The weekly plan for success should include tasks, the amount of time consumed by undertaking such tasks, and the number of times such tasks will be completed each week.

Working on individual tasks that form part of the overall project. makes things easier to control, easier to manoeuvre, and easier to adjust quickly if necessary. Smaller tasks are the building blocks of achievement, the threads in a bigger canvas. And the more coordinated they are, the more beautiful the canvas. All important things in life start with one small step. How we map these steps and move through them is what matters; I give more practical advice on this in the pages to come.

Ninth: doers and dreamers –
goals without actions are dreams

Objectives without actions are just thoughts. A brutal statement, but true. Reading this book may well be a sign you are ready to decide which one you prefer. To do or not to do? This is the question.

We often fail not because our goals are too big or too small, too complex or too simple, or because they take too long or we have too little time. Most of the time, we fail because we do not do the work that needs to be done. We do not do what is required to make something happen.

What it takes to make something happen is different from doing our best; it is simply doing what is required to get something done. Knowing where, how, and what to spend your time on is a start, but knowing and doing the tasks required to achieve your goals and knowing the time and amount of repetition to spend on tasks are all factors to your success ratios. Your time ratios will tell the truth.

Tenth: what counts

The importance of what we do has a different meaning for each of us, as each action does not hold the same relevance for all of us in general. Our lives have five parts – I call these the core five – which are the same for each of us. The value of each part varies from one another, which is what makes all of us different, yet the same. Find out what is important to you and to what degree. What you choose is what makes you who you are. Choose carefully, as your choices may not be undone.

What we do-in-time not only defines us but also defines the quality and success of our lives. The simple steps in this book offer a roadmap to success. Figuring out your current time ratios and adjusting your time ratios to achieve the desired results is a sure way to success. What it boils down to is a choice: do you choose to do it, or do you choose not to do it? A life-changing action starts and continues with a choice. What do you choose? This is the only question that counts.

CHAPTER 2

KNOW YOURSELF

'THE CENTRE OF YOUR LIFE IS YOU.'

"Watch your actions; they become your habits.
Watch your habits; they become your character.
Watch your character; it becomes your destiny."

— Lao Tzu

The foundation for your life journey is you. As the centre of your life is you, you are the only employee at your disposal to achieve your life objectives.

Knowing yourself is the foundation, framework, and driver of life. Not knowing yourself is to drift blindly; you cannot get anywhere by driving without seeing. Seeing from the inside out is the starting point of any meaningful journey. Life begins and ends with you; looking inward and knowing who you are is the foundation of all good things in life.

Knowing your strengths, weaknesses, ambitions, capabilities, pleasures, sources of sadness, motivations, demotivators, and what you stand for are all parts of self-knowing. Knowing those parts will help you overcome self-created challenges and take advantage of self-likes and feel-good actions. This involves navigating through emotions and thoughts – to be in control, not to be controlled.

I remember reading an article published by *Forbes* in March 2019. It said, 'Research shows that when we are more self-aware, we're more effective personally and professionally – able to make better decisions, be more confident and even build stronger relationships. And this extends across more spiritual, emotional, and mindful practices. All these practices teach us that understanding our inner world is the starting point for bringing about change. Yet research has also shown that although 95% of people think they are self-aware, only 10% to 15% are.'

How interesting! Our biggest challenges come from within ourselves, not from the outside world. We create hurdles, we stop ourselves from doing things, we make excuses, we are challenged by the priorities that we select, we work on assumptions most of the time and not on facts, and we are the ones who give up quickly. We care too much about what others think – particularly people around us. We rely too much on imposed limitations, and we interact with life without paying attention to what is going on. Research shows that more than sixty per cent of our daily actions are done without us thinking about them. We are on autopilot; our habits control us. We do not believe this, but it is true. Until we start paying attention to what we are doing, things will not change. There is a substantial difference between what we think we do, and what we do. We do not believe this, but it is real, and that is why the first step of knowing yourself is to write down what you do every day to track actions – not thoughts and conversations but true and real actions that you do in your time. This is where the journey to success starts.

Your life journey is you. You are the only employee that works for you. How does that employee of yours seem to be? Is she or he lazy, money-motivated, a doer, ambitious, a blamer, an excuse-maker, strong or weak? What kind of employee does your life have? You need to listen to yourself with your eyes, not your ears – remember, *it is not what you say; it is what you do.*

We let our thoughts, our perceptions, get the better of us. We are always busy, with no time for reflection, no space for taking a step back while looking at what we are doing, our daily lives moving at the speed of the internet, moments slipping through our fingers. But we still believe differently.

It is easier to believe something if it is exactly what we want to hear – but is it the truth? Listening with my eyes, which means looking at actions and not words, has changed my life personally and professionally. Listening with my eyes has given me a new, realistic outlook on myself and the people around me. I discovered that we say things to make us feel and look better in our own eyes and among others. I discovered most people speak words that don't convey the core truth; the truth in most conversations is a perception of facts. Listening with my eyes has given me the ability to look beyond words and define myself and others through actions. I no longer judge people on what they say only. I judge them on what they do and how much of what they say matches what they do. I look at my actions and not what I try to convince myself or others of.

Life is a project with two resources and one outcome that has endless possibilities. The two resources at your disposal are your time and your employee (you). The outcome of possibilities is determined by the efficiency of these two resources. The first resource, time, is one you have no control over. The other resource, the single employee in the project of your life, is the only one over which you have complete control. What will you do with these resources?

What kind of life do you want to have?

Knowing and understanding your capabilities, environment, restrictions, self-imposed constraints, and limitations are to know and understand how you will perform with the effort required to get things done. This understanding will give you the ability to plan around all the above-mentioned factors to produce high-quality results.

Questions to consider (and this is by no means all of them) are:
- What are you good at?
- What types of activity do you like, and dislike, the most?
- What actions satisfy your emotional needs?
- Where (how) do you spend the most time?
- How do you make decisions?
- What do you think of your own life?

The golden rule for projects

I mentioned earlier that any project has two resources. The outcomes of each project have endless possibilities depending on the three points of the golden triangle, as presented in Figure 1.

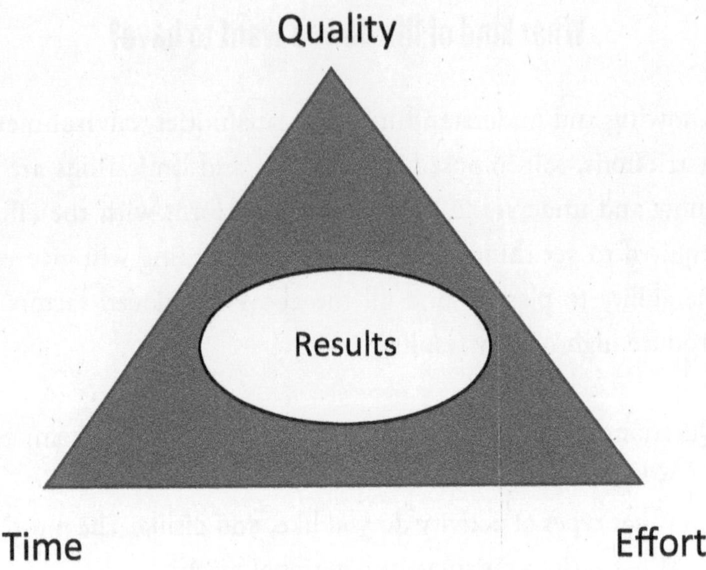

FIGURE 1. THE GOLDEN RULE FOR PROJECTS

All projects need duration to reach completion (time), and the work to be invested to reach subjective perfection (effort). The final piece of the triangle is the quality of the results. The results are at the centre of the triangle. Your life project is no different from the diagram. Think about any personal or professional project you are working on. What time do you have, and how much effort are you investing to get it done? Do you see a relationship between the amount of time spent and the effort invested in the quality of the results? Will the quality of results increase with the increase of time and effort spent in achieving the results?

The quality of the results depends on both resources, time and effort, together. The higher the quality, the more time and/or effort is needed. This takes us to two important questions when looking at the quality of what we are trying to achieve. Are your efforts of high quality? And are you doing enough to reach your desired results? Apply these questions to anything on which you are working on. They can be applied to any effort-results type of situation. Are you learning a new skill? What is the extent of your effort to learn? How often do you do it? Are you trying to lose weight? How is that working for you? Are you doing quality workouts in the gym? How often are you exercising? Be honest with yourself. If you are unable to give yourself desirable answers to these questions, then you must re-evaluate your way of getting your goals achieved.

Life is a continuous project. The quality of your life depends on the quality of the effort invested by your one employee – you – and the time invested in those efforts. This can all be summed up by what you do-in-time. This brings us full circle, back to knowing yourself. This is where it all starts. To know yourself is to know what that one life employee of yours is doing, when he/she is doing it, how often and for how long, what she/he can and cannot do, what her/his capabilities are, and knowing what to expect from her/him. That is the start.

Knowing yourself is not a challenging task to take on. It is about looking at and recording your actions with the time spent on those actions. It is to write down the truth, the facts, not the thoughts or proximities or assumptions, and to measure how and what consumes your time.

Your starting point – a daily inventory

Taking a daily inventory of your actions and feelings is the first and most crucial step to a successful life and the doorway to impressive results. Recording your daily activities with the time consumed and the effect those activities have on your emotions is the foundation of all the work to come.

Write down things that you do, small or big, things that take a long or brief time, in addition to regular activities like your daily commute to work and working hours. Write what you do and how long it takes to do daily tasks. Write down every small detail that has consumed time – nothing is too small – and do not take any activity lightly. In addition, having a description of the way you feel, start each activity, during the activity, and when you finish, will shed a light on your passions.

We are boxes of emotions, some darker than others. You need to peek into your box and know what you are working with. One straightforward way to do this is by the instant recording of what you do, reflecting on your actions and where they come from and why you did them. This will help you find your way to look inward to find out what is what.

You can record your activities in any way that works for you, so long as you capture the type of activities, the time spent on them, and your feelings throughout completing them. The control comes from gaining greater self-knowledge – for example, I was not happy at the gym, and only after recording my actions and my emotional state throughout those actions was I able to reach a breakthrough.

For any project with inadequate resources, one of two things will happen (or both). The quality will suffer, or it will take longer to get the desired results, or both. But how much time is allowed for your project life? For sure, it is not forever, and with time, as you get older, your life's one employee's capabilities change.

If the quality of the results is not important, then we can get away with investing less effort or less time, or both, to get the project done. Age is time; life is what you do in that time.

The golden triangle of project management can truncate in any way – but if you move one aspect (time, quality, or effort), it will always impact the others.

People might argue that life is not as simple as proposed here, that life is much more than what we do-in-time. To that I would say, my life results can only be tied to my efforts and nothing else. The fact that all of us have the same amount of time – 168 hours per week – makes life's playground, in a certain way, fair. We are all equal. Indeed, we do not all start at the same line or with the same opportunities, but that is what makes life more interesting, that is what makes us need each other, and that is where life changes hands, creating new opportunities for us to do-in-time things that can change the quality of our lives.

Take, for example, my childhood friends and me. For most of us, we had much in common. We came from the same neighbourhood, went to the same high school, and went on to the same college to complete the same majors, but we ended up in vastly different places in life. Many of them have not even left my hometown and still live in the same neighbourhood. While another friend comes from quite a wealthy neighbourhood, a private high school, a different social class, and studied a different major at the same university, I ended up doing better than him. It is a fact that our situations are not the same, which is true, but what we do-in-time while in those situations is what makes the difference. In my early career in the United States, two of the bosses that I worked for ended up working for me. Life is not constant; that is how life can change hands.

Most of the time, it's easy, and normal, to blame the way our lives proceed on others, like our parents, teachers, friends, or the situation more broadly. We blame luck, the universe, and everything else in between to avoid blaming ourselves. The pain of facing our truth has an agonising effect.

How do you think people become champions, elite performers, and icons of success? It is not through excuses but through consistent genuine efforts.

The projection problem

We use self-projection constantly as a defence mechanism for our internal self to defend against negative parts of ourselves. The same can be said for unwanted traits, denying they exist in us by blaming others or blaming external circumstances but not ourselves, by attributing our poor achievements to other things, both people and situations. Self-discovery is the opposite of self-projection. It is to know and bear the responsibility of doing something and its results.

It's important to recognise your strength is your difference. You can only know this by observing your actions and by considering what you do and do not do. Your actions truly tell who you are. You will discover yourself by catching yourself in the act, not in what you imagine yourself doing. Self-knowledge is the centre of self-doing, digging below the surface to discover one's reality forms the framework that you must work your plans within. Take time to ask yourself, 'How well do I know myself? What drives me? What is it I do with time?'

People fail because they think about the results and not the work or the worker. They do not consider the process, which is how they are going to get it done, and instead, they think about the what, not the how. We focus on results and fail to focus our efforts on what we do-in-time to get the results. Success should be measured by performing the efforts as planned, and by what we do-in-time. When genuine efforts are expended, results follow.

Self-knowing exercises are simple in nature, and while they require little effort and time, they need to be followed with persistence and consistency. The simplest exercise, as mentioned earlier, is keeping a daily journal of all your actions, small or big, with the time spent on each action, each day, taking an inventory of your day, every day. You need to record any given action that you have done, the amount of time spent on it, and how you felt before you started, while you were doing it, and when you finished doing it. Examining your reactions to what you have done during the day by reviewing recorded emotions will give you an honest insight into what you like and dislike, while the time spent on each action will indicate how you are truly spending your time. It will become clear after a few weeks what matters to you along with what does not, why some things get done faster and others slower or not at all, and which activities bring you joy or agonise you.

This simple act of keeping a daily journal can do wonders for your success, your future, and your life. If acted upon with belief, it will lead to an 'elite ship', as I call it. But make no mistake, this is not a secret formula deep inside of us. It is simply a method used through the ages that can be summarised in the following paragraph:

To achieve any goal, big or small, you need to expend the necessary effort for as long as required to complete the task properly. Free yourself from distractions and any activities that do not serve the achievement of your goal. When you are feeling energised, do more, and when you feel depleted, do the minimum. Select your goals with your mind and your heart. Keep going and only turn back to learn, measure, and adjust. Becoming an elite in any subject takes consistency and persistence. Face yourself at the start of your journey, not at the end.

Start your journal today; start it now. Take a daily inventory in the evening of all the things that you have done during that day and how long each activity took. This daily inventory will tell you what actions are wasting your time. Every day, write a simple journal using whatever means are available to you, so long as you get it done.

The next chapter will offer more direction on monitoring, making, and reading the daily journal, while enjoying the path to becoming a remarkable success.

CHAPTER 3
MONITOR

LISTEN WITH YOUR EYES.

*"Your choices define your actions;
your actions define your life."*

— Debasish Mridha

What we do defines us, not what we say. As the great proverb tells us, actions speak louder than words. This is the first and most crucial step in discovering yourself and discovering your ratio to success. It starts with recording your daily actions without any sugar-coating or prejudice. Just record what you do, with the start and finish time, to know the amount of time spent on each action.

You can use any means available to you. You can use your mobile phone with voice memos, notes, emails, or any other way that is easy for you. Recording can be done action by action, day by day, or once a week if you have a good memory, which I do not advise as information tends to become vague and inaccurate.

The idea is to record your actions as accurately as possible in order to have true and honest results. You may know the saying, 'garbage in, garbage out'; that is the type of result you will have if the entries are not accurate. The evidence, as mentioned in the *Harvard Business Review*, is clear. People are not at all accurate in self-evaluating their time-management proficiency. The recording needs to be done for a minimum of eight weeks. My recommendation is to do it for sixteen weeks at this stage. You will discover a stark difference between what is real and what is self-perception.

Having some knowledge of Microsoft Excel is a good thing for working out your success ratio but not necessary; some basic calculations can be done manually. Once actions have been recorded daily, ideally, they should be transferred into an Excel spreadsheet or a table.

You might ask, 'What things should be recorded, and how often do I need to record them?'

Before answering this question, we need to be as detailed as we can in our recording to attain accurate results. Remember, the results are yours to own, no one else's. No one should see any of it; this information is meant for you only.

Again, before answering the questions above, you need to understand why you need to record all your daily actions, small or large, with the start and finish times. The answer for most people is this: daily activities are common routines. They are completed in a manner akin to an autopilot mode. They come from the subconscious, and it is hard to admit that. Understanding that what you achieve in life is directly connected to your actions, how can you know what you will achieve if more than sixty per cent of your actions happen without any idea about them? If they just happen and keep on happening? Achieving happens with deliberate actions.

Great life achievements are the results of actions. Actions start with a choice. Some people are more disciplined than others and more self-aware and shift into action as they can see the road ahead to their intended results. They build their routines around the actions needed to achieve their goals, and some of them reach the point of obsession. They are on autopilot, a good autopilot, after creating a deliberate routine that is designed around achieving results, getting things done, taking care of business, not wasting time, and avoiding distractions. This book is not for them; this book is for anyone who wants to succeed.

You may have already noticed that the term 'do-in-time' is in most paragraphs of this book. This is to emphasise the point that the deciding factor of success is what you do-in-time and how genuine you are in doing it. Time and effort are the only two factors to achieving anything; time and effort are equal to success.

What do you spend your time on? Sleeping, working, commuting, learning, developing, travelling, or scrolling through the internet? How many of your total 168 weekly hours remain for other things? It's not that we forget all days are made of twenty-four hours. Instead, we do not consider the fact that during this time, life continues to happen, and a few years later, you are where you are. The difference with the result, successful or otherwise, is what we do-in-time – we are all given the same amount of time.

To help ourselves be successful while doing everyday things, we need a tool, a way, a method, or anything to help us understand and realise how to get there. Such a tool is as simple as writing down what you do every day in as much detail as possible. As outlined in Table 1, write down the type of activity and the start and finish times, to calculate how much time is spent on each activity. Then calculate all the time spent on doing activities for each week. We will use the week as our time block; a day is too short, and a month is too long. See below for an example of the diary method.

Action	Start Time	Finish Time	Total Time	Feeling
Getting ready for work	6:30 a.m.	7:00 a.m.	30 minutes	rushed
Breakfast	7:00 a.m.	7:15 a.m.	15 minutes	good
Commuting to work	7:15 a.m.	7:55 a.m.	40 minutes	stressed
Work	8:00 a.m.	5:30 p.m.	9 hours, 30 minutes	okay

TABLE 1. DIARY FORMAT FOR RECORDING DAILY ACTIVITIES

The secret to getting the recording done is to make it as easy as possible by utilising what is available to you all the time. You can use your phone, your computer, voice memos, or write notes or emails to yourself. Any method that fits your lifestyle is fine. The question we are trying to answer is what we do-in-time and the amount of time it consumes. We are trying to determine what we do with our most valuable resource – time.

In addition, this method will help you to know yourself better by keeping annotations next to each activity, such as what your feelings were at that time. A simple notation is enough.

You need to keep recording for a minimum of eight weeks; it is good to continue for longer than sixteen weeks, and it is excellent to keep on doing it for longer. You will use the findings in your daily time inventories to discover yourself. The heart of this whole book lies in this exercise. Accuracy in as much recording as possible needs to be emphasised, so that the picture we create from the results is true and accurate, which is required to understand and act upon our actions. You do not want to cheat yourself; the worst kind of cheating is when we direct it inwards.

This is not about time management

Let us be clear – this is not a 'to-do' list. We are not trying to do more with the same amount of time; we are simply keeping a record of what we spend our time on and how much time is consumed to do it. The diary entry is recorded after the action is done, while time-management tools are for use before the action is done. That is where those tools fail most of the time – they do not consider what you are doing, and how you are doing it. They have no clue of what you like or do not like and are based on your predetermined thoughts and ideas, which, for most of us, are not factual.

Recording what you have done and how long it took is collecting data about your daily actions and routines. It is the first step in data analysis; we will look at what you are doing and what you should be doing based on your goals. It is a gap analysis, which is a standard procedure in an improvement process. If you are going to improve your life, you need to know where you are now, where you need to be, and what actions are required to close the gap in between.

Recording actions every day can be dull, boring, and, in some cases, an overwhelming task. The good news is that it is easier than ever before with today's technology at your fingertips. With the constant development of mobile phones and apps, our lives are changing, our habits are changing, and our time consumption is changing.

Come to think of it, the mobile phone is the most powerful tool ever created by humankind. Take advantage of it by making it work for you. Once a week, transfer those records into your journal for weekly calculations; treat your mobile phone as your timekeeping machine. For your journal, it can be a simple table, an Excel spreadsheet, a Word document, or whatever works for you. Start using your mobile phone now for recording your daily activities, and use voice memos, notes, or any other app that you like.

This is not to say that tracking your every action every day is not a challenge. It can be, but it is an easy challenge. All that it takes is a choice and a bit of discipline. It does not have to be perfect; it doesn't have to be one hundred per cent accurate. But it should be as close to the truth as possible, as you want to get true results. Being true to yourself is assessed through this documentation. You are not answering to anyone with this but yourself. You are doing it for yourself. It is your truth; be incredibly careful what you tell yourself. Create a table or a calendar or a schedule-type of sheet. Many online sources can provide any of these items for free such as www.calendarpedia.com. Use these for keeping your information somewhere retrievable.

It is more effective to use the style of Table 2. This will enable you to capture the required information while keeping the information type and time spent on the activity simple.

Date _____________________ Day _____________________					
Activity	Activity category	Start time	Finish time	Total time	My feelings

TABLE 2. WEEKLY ACTIVITIES AND THE TIME SPENT ON EACH

1. On a piece of paper in a notebook (you can use a mobile phone, tablet, or computer), create six columns for the daily calendar, titled Date and a then the column titled, Activity, Activity type or category Start time, Finish time, Total time, and how you felt during the activities.
2. Fill out the table by writing down each activity or action taken during each day of the week including the weekend; do not leave anything out. Then repeat this for every day of the week.
3. Put the date above and the day of the week next to it.
4. In the Activity column, write a few words that describe the activity or action.
5. Select the Activity category from one of the examples in Table 3. If the task or activity is not in any of the categories listed, put it under 'Other'. If the activity is repeated more than once a week, then give it a new category name and carry it forward.
6. In the Start and Finish columns, write the time you started and the time you finished. For ease of recording, use your mobile or voice record your notice with as much detail as you can. Then transfer that information into the spreadsheet when you can. Do not delay, as procrastination is the invisible enemy.
7. On the following day, add up all the time you spent on each category. At the end of the week, add the hours spent on each category using the above schedule (Table 2) but for weekly totals.

Category	Activities
Sleep	
Work	
Commuting	
Family time	Taking care of family member
	Spending time with family
	Attending kids' functions
	Household activities
Learning and development	Gym, reading, training, education
Leisure and relaxing	Socializing, movies, theatre, recreation
Mobile and internet	Tablets, computers, social media
Personal care	Grooming, doctor visits
Eating and drinking	Including food preparation
Travel	
Other	

TABLE 3. EXAMPLES OF ACTIVITY CATEGORIES

Write the activity and the category to which it belongs. For example, shaving is an activity that belongs to the Personal care category. Driving to work belongs to the Commuting category. Preparing food for friends belongs to the Eating and drinking category.

To summarise again, fill out the form by writing down each activity, describing in a few words the category in which it falls, the start and finish times, what your feelings are. If you cannot figure out the answer for the last item, do not worry. It will become clearer with time. Do this for each day of each week including the weekends; do not leave anything out. Then repeat it for a minimum of eight weeks. Mark the top of each table with dates and the day for each week and have them organised in a time sequence.

You can have as many categories as you like. If the category is not listed, you can create a new one.

At the end of the week, add up the hours spent on each category using Table 3. Your time totals will be for every week. The daily totals will be carried forward at the end of each week to produce a weekly total. The weekly time block is the most effective block for measuring time spent on activities. The days can be unique, such as weekend days, holidays, and days off, whereas the week has all-day types in it including workdays and weekends. The monthly block is too long and is a repetition of the weekly block. In addition, some weeks will overlap with successive months.

Looking at Table 3, some of the categories include sleep, work, commuting, family time, learning and development, leisure and relaxation, personal care, eating, drinking, travel, and others, along with mobile and internet use, which is the fastest-growing time-consumption category of humankind. You will see that some category types are constant. You can organise these categories in any order you like. There is no preference, no priority. Arrange them any way you like.

Many people talk about time, and so many books refer to time-related issues. Books talk about time in diverse ways. I would like to talk about time as if it is money. Now, if you think about time like money, our perspectives and outlook on time will differ. Each day, at midnight, your time account is credited with 1,440 minutes for you to use. If this translated to $1,440 losing one dollar every minute, how would you use it? How would you use the balance? You cannot carry this amount forward because at midnight the following day, the balance will reset to zero, and then it starts all over again. You cannot have an overdraft or draw against the future balance. What you do not use, the bank will simply wipe off your account. That is your time, and you read zero as we reach the next strike of midnight. Every midnight, you are credited back with 1,440 minutes, and on it goes like that.

If you fail to use this deposit, there will be no going back, and no borrowing against tomorrow. Once it is gone, it is gone. Yesterday is the past, tomorrow is no guarantee, and only now is what you have – make it count.

Bringing consciousness to action

We are not always conscious of our actions. This is the way that humans have been created and the way we operate. It has been human nature from the start of Creation that we perform as creatures of habit. We do not like the unknown; familiarity feels safe to us. We hate pain, we avoid confrontation, especially with ourselves, and we resist change. Monitoring our actions does not conflict with human nature. It does not ask for things to change. It simply asks us to watch our actions, to be aware, and to discover the gap between reality and perception.

In this chapter, you start with your own reality, the truth of who you are, by discovering where you spend your efforts and what you do-in-time, the time that forms your life. The truth is the opposite of self-deception. This can only happen by watching and confirming our actual actions, overcoming self-biases about our efforts and life, and validating what is true. Without tracking what we do-in-time, you and I and everyone else remain biased about our beliefs and ideas of ourselves. We are biased about what and how we think and dismiss thoughts that conflict with such conformations. Taking a step backwards to take two steps forward is much better than taking no steps at all. Staying in your comfort zone will lead to no progress because it does not require any change. It is familiar, and we love familiarity.

Beginning in the 1960s, psychologists such as Robert Zajonc, Charles Goetzinger, Robert Bornstein, and others have shown that people tend to develop preferences for things simply because they are familiar with them. In a 1968 piece in the *Journal of Personality and Social Psychology Monograph Supplement*, Robert Zajonc reported on a mysterious student who had been attending a class at Oregon State University for the past two months enveloped in a big black bag. Only his bare feet were showing. Each Monday, Wednesday, and Friday at 11 a.m., the black bag entered the classroom and sat on a small table near the back. The class was Speech 113 – Basic Persuasion. Charles Goetzinger, the professor of the class, knew the identity of the person inside. None of the twenty students in the classroom did. At first, the students treated the black bag with hostility, which, over time, turned into curiosity and, eventually, friendship. Why do you think companies keep pounding advertisements in your face? Repetition creates familiarity.

Collecting data with the intent to analyse and understand what you do-in-time is the desired result of this activity. It is not an analysis of your skills or capabilities to figure out your chances of succeeding. Rather, it is about knowing how much of your available time you need to spend to achieve success. It is like having an open book test on life; the answers are in front of you. The answers you are looking for are in the next chapter, the Discovery chapter, which will tell you all you need to know about your time consumption and your time ratios.

CHAPTER 4

DISCOVERY

PERCEPTION OF REALITY IS NOT REALITY.

"Time is what we want most, but what we use worst."

— William Penn

You have recorded what you did all day and night; you added up the hours for each category. Your total weekly hours are 168 hours a week – what consumes your time? Are the numbers what you thought they would be?

Work, sleep, spending time with family, learning, and leisure are what you do-in-time. This is the same for most of us, regardless of where we come from. We tend to think of time as a space with us in it.

The truth is we and our time are the same. We no longer exist when our time expires; we are over once our clock stops. People are the most intelligent form of independent life, but we do the most ridiculous things and misuse the most precious thing that we have.

The confirmation-bias trap

In his book, *18 Minutes*, Peter Bregman talks about how we confuse our expectations of reality with reality itself. He identified that our desire for facts is a desire for our own facts and not the truth. We look for evidence and signs to confirm what we believe in, which Bregman identifies as 'confirmation bias'.

Confirmation bias is the bed of comfort. Our bias stops us from admitting to what we do not like. It gives us the okay for the way we are, what we do, and the way we feel. It makes us feel good about ourselves and keeps us from wanting change. It also gives us the illusion that we are doing what needs to be done. *When we face failure, we create excuses.* Confirmation bias comes running to support the reasoning for excuses; excuses make us escape the pain of reality. We stay in our comfort zone, where it is familiar, and we do not have to change. This gives us a sense of control.

Knowing your biases is the natural outcome of recording your everyday actions. You do not have to do more than accurately record your actions. This information will show you the deception.

What do people do-in-time?

According to the Organisation for Economic Co-operation and Development (OECD; see also Figure 2), a recent survey shows that most people spend a total of 8.3 hours per day sleeping, and about 7.45 hours a day working, with some variation among the different criteria. Time spent on the internet is 6.3 hours per day, of which 2.24 hours per day is spent on social media. Combined, these activities total around 22.46 hours per day. The remaining 1.14 hours each day are allotted to all the other activities, including family time, learning and development, eating and drinking, seeing friends, housework, shopping, exercising, reading, and any other tasks.

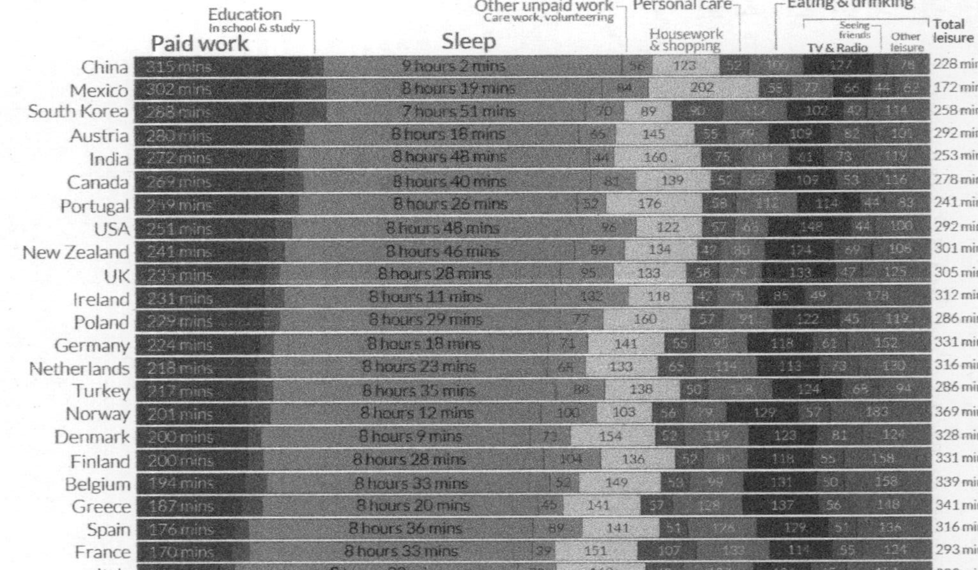

FIGURE 2. CHART OF HOW PEOPLE SPEND THEIR TIME (SOURCE: HTTPS://OURWORLDINDATA.ORG)

Most people surveyed by the OECD said they used the internet for less than three hours a day, without checking their mobile phones or computers for confirmation. That is what they believed and what they operated on. But actual research shows that the same people used the internet for more than 6.3 hours a day, double the time that they believed. Where did this discrepancy come from? Internet use of 6.3 hours per day equates to more than forty-four hours per week. With 168 hours in a week, the internet use for the average person consumes more than twenty-six per cent of their total weekly hours. When factoring in the average sleeping time of fifty-six hours per week, this leaves 112 hours for all other things to do. When factoring in the only other available hours in a week, after deducting sleeping hours, this adjusts internet usage to more than thirty-nine per cent of an average person's waking hours.

The modern conundrum

Here is a problem that I see everywhere. We are consumed with doing things to the point of our maximum capacity but are getting the least done – doing and getting things done are two different outcomes. More than ever, we are using our brains in a million separate ways, while becoming more technology dependent. Our brains are storing images and ideas, but our memories are getting shorter and shorter. Things are happening so fast that our behaviours are changing rapidly. It is a race. Days fly by, and in the blink of an eye, you are twenty, thirty, or fifty years old and wondering, 'Where did all those years go?' Then time stops; it is over.

This is not intended as a dark and gloomy outlook on life. It is life at its best these days – it is reality. No matter how much we hate to admit it or think about it, changes keep on coming, and evolution keeps happening at a faster pace. This is how life works – faster and faster – and we cannot keep up from inception to the end. Understanding this will have the biggest impact on the quality of our lives before and after the end of our time. Shifting one's thinking from time passing to doing-in-time is the highest level of living.

Most precious... But...

You keep track of your money, bank account, cheques, deductions, transfers, and deposits. Transactions are reconciled, and what you end up with is your daily bank-account balance. Which is the amount of funds that are available to you in the bank. You would go crazy if any of your money went missing! The daily bank-account balance is the net result of money flowing in and out of your account. Together, they make cash flow. Without proper records, you cannot keep accurate track of your money. For a fee or something in return, someone else can help you with that, namely banks; with technology, it's easier than ever. Who is helping you to reconcile your time? Unless you fundamentally believe that time is more valuable than money, nothing will change. Harvey Mackay says, 'Time is free, but it is priceless. You cannot own it, but you can use it. You cannot keep it, but you can spend it. Once you have lost it, you can never get it back.'

It will not happen if you try to withdraw money from your bank account without sufficient funds. If you write cheques without funds, those cheques will be worthless. You might even get into trouble for writing those cheques. You can only withdraw what you have, not a penny more. Every night at midnight, your time account is credited with 1,440 minutes for you to use within the next twenty-four hours. That is the full start-up balance every midnight.

There are three differences between a money account and a time account, making time the most valuable resource known to humankind. These are:

1. Your time account is reduced by the second.
2. No one can add any more to their time account.
3. Others can safely keep your money, but no one can safely keep your time.

When it comes to your time, you are the banker, the keeper, the controller, the cashier, the manager, the burglar, the embezzler, and the customer – it is all you. Time not used is time wasted, sucked into space – nothing time is stolen time. Stop and look.

Starting at midnight, your account is full of 1,440 minutes. Now let's break this down.

Twenty-four hours in each day comprising sixty minutes each (24*60 = 1,440), your time account is full. You can set your starting point at any time other than midnight; just keep in mind that the starting time is also the finishing time. It is a full circle. If your starting time is set at 6 a.m., then your finish time is 5:59 a.m. the next day – a full twenty-four hours.

For the sake of the exercise, we will take our daily tracking activities from the previous chapter and convert all time tracked from hours into minutes.

As stated earlier, people sleep on average eight hours and thirty-one minutes per day. When converted to minutes, this is eight hours multiplied by sixty minutes each hour equals four hundred eighty minutes plus thirty-one minutes equals five hundred eleven minutes of sleeping per day. People work seven hours and forty-six minutes per day, which is seven hours multiplied by sixty minutes equals four hundred twenty minutes plus forty-six minutes equals four hundred sixty six minutes per day. Internet time is six hours and thirty minutes per day (av.), which is six hours multiplied by sixty minutes equals three hundred sixty minutes plus thirty minutes equals three hundred ninety minutes per day. If you want to break this down further, out of those six hours and thirty minutes of internet time, two hours and twenty-four minutes are on social media, which equates to one hundred forty four minutes per day. Following these figures, our daily time balance can be expressed in the following way.

Item	Start Balance	Used	Remaining Balance
	1,440		
Sleep		511	929
Work		466	463
Internet		390	73

TABLE 4. AVERAGE TIME USE PER DAY

We can see from Table 4 that if you subtract work, sleep, and internet time from your day, you have a remaining seventy-three minutes for all the other activities. This is only one hour and thirteen minutes. Some might argue that these numbers are not accurate. They may be right. Activities overlap in time; for example, internet time is part of work or entertainment. People on average check their mobile phones ninety six times per day. But it should be noted that we didn't include all activities in this exercise, such as commuting to and from work, family time, and entertainment time. Another reason people think these numbers are not correct is because of confirmation bias.

To keep things simple for now, we will continue with the above numbers. The five hundred eleven minutes that we use to sleep out of the one thousand four hundred forty minutes forms 35.5% of our total available time: five hundred eleven minutes divided by one thousand four hundred forty multiplied by 100% = 35.5%, leaving us with 100% – 35.5% = 64.5% of our remaining time.

The four hundred sixty six minutes spent at work, out of one thousand four hundred forty minutes, is 32.4% of our total available time: four hundred sixty six divided by one thousand four hundred forty multiplied by 100% = 32.4%, leaving us with 100% – 32.4% = 67.6%. Sleeping and working consume more than 67.9% (35.5% + 32.4%) of daily available time, which leaves us with 32.1% (100% – 67.9%). Now, internet time is (390/1,440 X 100% = 27%), and once that is added to sleep and work (67.9% + 27%), it will make up 94.9% of our total daily available time. The remainder of our time balance (100% – 94.9%) is 5.10%, which is seventy-three minutes!

The above may not be accurate in all cases, but it is a close enough estimation. You will discover your numbers once you start tracking your activities. Or your bias will convince you otherwise. With seventy-three minutes a day, how can you get anything done?

In 2018, the National Institute of Health (NIH) funded a study. A group of researchers from Duke University, Pennington Biomedical Research Centre, and Johns Hopkins University, among others, undertook a different approach to weight-loss research that included more than 1,700 overweight people.

The researchers asked half the group of participants to write down everything they ate during the day; the other half of the group was asked to do nothing. It was not easy at the beginning for the first group of participants to record all the information about what they ate daily. Some participants forgot their recording journals. Some would snack but forget to write down what they ate between meals. Other times, they could not even remember these instances. Slowly, participants learned to properly track their daily food intake and keep better records. Their recording methods improved with time, and some participants were keeping detailed daily food-consumption records. Participants started looking at their records, finding patterns they had no idea about. They had never thought about them before, and it was like seeing them for the first time. The study found that the simple act of recording food-consumption activities helped twice as much in losing weight as not keeping records.

The simple act of writing down what they ate encouraged people to consume fewer calories, as claimed by the lead researcher, Jack Hollis (PhD). The simple act of recording time consumed in each activity will help you to better use your time. It will give you the opportunity to know for sure without any bias what you do-in-time. It will open your eyes to habits that you do not know that you have. It will give you a peek inside your subconscious, revealing what makes you do or not do things, and what makes you feel good or bad. The simple act of recording what you do-in-time can double your chances to achieve your goals without doing much more than this.

Good decisions come from true and accurate information

Proper decisions stem from true and accurate information. We are living now in the age of information; information is available at our fingertips about anything you can think of. But not about ourselves. Meanwhile, others collect our information with every click and swipe we make. We need to start collecting information about our actions. This simple act will open windows into our thoughts and feelings and the choices that drive those actions that define us, the quality of our lives, and our legacy at the end.

What happens when you watch a movie while constantly distracted by so many things and so much noise around you? What happens if you watch the same movie for a second time, without distraction? It's like seeing it for the first time. This is what the recording of our every activity every day will do for us. You will be watching your life movie without distraction from a true angle. It shows the details of which you are unaware. It is easy to get off track without realising it. Things sneak up on you every day from inside and outside, all kinds of things – trivial things, important things, bad things, and good things. New things will take over. Other things will become lost or shovelled around.

Priorities change – you get tired, you get busy, you sink in, and habits and routines take over.

The perception of what you are doing with your life is not what you are doing with your life. Prove to yourself that you are doing the things that will take you where you want to go. Targeted achievement is the destination. Actions are the journey to reach that destination. Tracking what you do-in-time is the first action in that journey. Your actions are the vessel that will carry you to success. You remain the captain of that vessel. Knowing what goes on that vessel every day guarantees a successful journey, long or short. Equip your vessel in the best way that suits your needs. As the captain, you steer that ship whichever way you choose, knowing your time consumption is the dashboard of your ship. Without a dashboard, you cannot have a sense of direction or speed or be aware of faults within your ship. Without a dashboard, you are sailing blind. Good luck getting to where you are going.

Every week, add up your timesheets for each of the categories, and study and consider the time spent. What are your top-time consumers? Is time spent doing valuable actions? What actions or activities are time-wasters? Is the time you spend on achieving your goals of high or low ratios? Knowing how and on what you spend your time is important before jumping into the next chapter. We are about to learn the benefits of the time ratio and what it means for your life.

CHAPTER 5
WHAT IS YOUR RATIO?

MY TIME, MY LIFE.

"It is not enough to be busy. So are the ants.
The question is: What are we busy about?"

— Henry David Thoreau

Numbers do not lie, people do. The most dangerous proposition is when we lie to ourselves, which we do all the time.

This book will not discuss where and how your habits formed or came from. Its purpose is to give you a formula for success based on facts and numbers. It is a well-known fact that humans are creators of habits. In a research paper published by Duke University in 2006, it was found that more than sixty per cent of people performed actions every day without making any actual decisions about those actions. They were performed through habit. Habits become engraved in our internal systems without full awareness. Additionally, habits form over different time lengths for varied reasons. Many studies have been performed over the years to learn more about human actions, habits, internal thoughts, psychology, and social behaviour to discover various aspects of ourselves. In most of these studies, it was clear that people are complex creatures mentally, emotionally, and socially. Other studies suggested that people are simple and that humans are fascinating creatures.

Think about it. When sixty per cent of our daily actions are habits, this means we do not fully consider such actions; we just do them. This means that we are not truly aware of what we do-in-time and that we do not know for sure how our time is being consumed. If part of your daily habit is wasting time, then that time should be considered as leaked time, as wasted time!

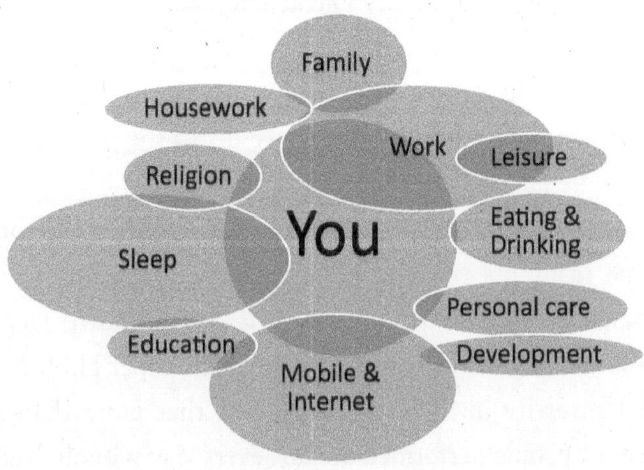

FIGURE 3. THE NORMAL SET OF ACTIVITIES UNDERTAKEN EACH DAY

Daily activities

Let us look at what this activity cloud looks like for you. Take an inventory of your daily activities, both routine and non-routine. Do your best to list all activities regardless of size or repetition with a focus on the routine ones. Table 5 provides an example of a normal day for the average person with the start, end, and total time spent on each activity. The total time for all actions cannot be more than twenty-four hours. If the time has passed with no activities, it should be included in the table with a 'no activities' column. For accurate dashboard reading and analysis, your tracking should be like that shown in Table 5. It does not have to be the same or show the same order of items; you can list as many activities as you like in the order you like. It will be easier to use, and the daily table should mirror the weekly table. It will be much easier if both tables are created in Excel spreadsheets.

In an Excel spreadsheet (see Table 5):

1. Create a table with seven columns.
2. The first column is daily activities (type and name).
3. The second column is the start time of that activity.
4. The third column is the finish time of that activity.
5. The fourth column is the number of hours spent doing that activity.
6. The fifth column is the number of minutes used in that activity when it is not whole hours. If the amount of time

spent is in whole hours, then the total value of this column will be zero.

7. The sixth column is for the total time used in hours. This can be calculated by dividing the number of minutes by sixty (minutes in one hour) and adding these to the hours from the fourth column, if any.

8. The seventh column is to multiply the number of hours in the sixth column by sixty minutes (minutes in one hour and then added to the minutes from the fifth column).

9. You do not need both hours and minutes columns. One is enough so long as you do it the same way for daily and weekly tracking sheets, while making sure the hour column adds up to twenty-four hours and the minute column adds up to 1,440 minutes. If the total is not twenty-four hours (1,440 minutes), go back and check all numbers entered, making sure they are accurate.

Monday						
Daily Activities	Start Time	Finish Time	Time Used		Total Time Used in	Total Time Used in
			Hours	Minutes	Hours	Minutes
Sleep	22:00	6:00	8	0	8.00	480
shower/ dress	6:05	6:45	0	40	0.67	40
breakfast	6:45	7:00	0	20	0.33	20
Family	7:05	7:40	0	35	0.58	35
commute to	7:40	8:25	0	45	0.75	45
work	8:30	18:00	9	30	9.50	570
commute back	18:00	18:55	0	55	0.92	55
Eat & drink	19:00	19:40	0	40	0.92	55
Relax -family	19:40	21:00	1	20	1.33	80
Read - mobile	21:00	21:50	0	50	0.83	50
Personal Care	21:50	22:00	0	10	0.17	10
Total					24.00	1,440

TABLE 5. EXAMPLE ALLOTMENT OF TIME SPENT ON ACTIVITIES

When it comes to routine, all days in a week are not the same. Even if you like to keep going non-stop, your body will not let you. Natural abilities can be pushed, but only to a certain limit. To create the weekly ratio table (you can call it anything you like – timetable, activities table, etc.), transfer the daily time consumed for each day and mirror the daily sheet for all seven days of the week.

Daily time consumption does not give the complete picture of what you do-in-time. For most people, weekdays are not the same as weekends or days off; we do different activities on the weekend and days off compared to workdays.

My ratio?

A ratio is defined as the quantitative relation between two amounts, showing the number of times one value is contained within the other.

Our time block is a week, which comprises 10,080 minutes – no more, no less. The ratio is how much time is consumed by one activity from the whole 10,080 minutes per week. For example, in Table 6, time spent sleeping is 31.3 per cent of your weekly time. That is, about one-third of the week is consumed by sleep alone, while 26.6 per cent of the weekly time is spent at work. Those two activities consume more than half of your total weekly time. All other activities consume less than half of all available weekly time.

This dashboard will tell you what you are doing in time and if your efforts are aligned to serving your goals and objectives. Table 6 is easy to understand and easy to copy. Start calculating your weekly time ratios now. Find out where your minutes are getting sucked away.

	weekly Ratios								
Activities	Monday	Tuesday	Wednesday	Thursday	Friday	Saturday	Sunday	Total	Weekly Ratio
	Minutes Used	Minutes Used	Minutes Used	Minutes Used	Minutes Used	Minutes Used	Minutes Used	Minutes Used	
Sleep	480	450	420	420	480	420	480	3150	31.3%
shower/ dress	45	20	20	35	30	30	40	220	2.2%
breakfast	25	30	20	20	15	10	30	150	1.5%
News & updates	35	45	40	20	45	30	10	225	2.2%
commute to	45	40	40	45	40	55	50	315	3.1%
work	575	500	510	515	0	0	580	2680	26.6%
commute back	55	50	45	50	45	30	50	325	3.2%
Eat & drink	20	10	10	75	75	90	10	290	2.9%
Relax -family	10	15	10	15	30	80	15	175	1.7%
Mobile - Social Media	140	125	115	140	235	235	110	1100	10.9%
Personal Care	10	20	20	20	45	30	20	165	1.6%

TV & Internet	0	60	60	75	90	90	0	375	3.7%
GYM & Sports	0	0	60	0	60	60	0	180	1.8%
Personal Development	0	30	30	0	60	60	15	195	1.9%
House activities	0	45	0	10	80	120	30	285	2.8%
Travel	0	0	0	0	0	0	0	0	0.0%
friends & Entertainment	0	0	40	0	110	100	0	250	2.5%
Total	1440	1440	1440	1440	1440	1440	1440	10080	100%

TABLE 6. AVERAGE WEEKLY ALLOTMENT OF TIME (MINUTES) SPENT ON ACTIVITIES

weekly Ratios									
Activities	Monday Hours Used	Tuesday Hours Used	Wednesday Hours Used	Thursday Hours Used	Friday Hours Used	Saturday Hours Used	Sunday Hours Used	Total Hours Used	Weekly Ratio
Sleep	8.0	7.5	7.0	7.0	8.0	7.0	8.00	52.5	31.3%
shower/ dress	0.8	0.3	0.3	0.6	0.5	0.5	0.67	3.7	2.2%
breakfast	0.4	0.5	0.3	0.3	0.3	0.2	0.50	2.5	1.5%
News & updates	0.6	0.8	0.7	0.3	0.8	0.5	0.17	3.8	2.2%
commute to	0.8	0.7	0.7	0.8	0.7	0.9	0.83	5.3	3.1%
work	9.6	8.3	8.5	8.6	0.0	0.0	9.67	44.7	26.6%
commute back	0.9	0.8	0.8	0.8	0.8	0.5	0.83	5.4	3.2%
Eat & drink	0.3	0.2	0.2	1.3	1.3	1.5	0.17	4.8	2.9%
Relax -family	0.2	0.3	0.2	0.3	0.5	1.3	0.25	2.9	1.7%
Mobile - Social Media	2.3	2.1	1.9	2.3	3.9	3.9	1.83	18.3	10.9%
Personal Care	0.2	0.3	0.3	0.3	0.8	0.5	0.33	2.8	1.6%
TV & Internet	0.0	1.0	1.0	1.3	1.5	1.5	0.00	6.3	3.7%

GYM & Sports	0.0	0.0	1.0	0.0	1.0	1.0	0.00	3.0	1.8%
Personal Development	0.0	0.5	0.5	0.0	1.0	1.0	0.25	3.3	1.9%
House activities	0.0	0.8	0.0	0.2	1.3	2.0	0.50	4.8	2.8%
Travel	0.0	0.0	0.0	0.0	0.0	0.0	0.00	0.0	0.0%
friends & Entertainment	0.0	0.0	0.7	0.0	1.8	1.7	0.00	4.2	2.5%
Total	24	24	24	24	24	24	24	168	100%

TABLE 7. AVERAGE WEEKLY ALLOTMENT OF TIME (HOURS) SPENT ON ACTIVITIES

It might be easier for you to see your time ratios in hours, not minutes, as we are more accustomed to hours. Table 6 is in minutes, while Table 7 is presented in hours. The ratios are the same for both; it is just that hours are more familiar to most people. Take a closer look at both tables.

How to read the numbers

What do those numbers mean? They mean that sleeping consumed one-third of your weekly time, and work consumed more than twenty-five per cent of your weekly time, while more than ten per cent of your total weekly time was spent on mobile and/or social media, with almost ten per cent of your weekly time eating, drinking, and performing house activities. If we consider sleeping time as not being available time to use, then the ratios change significantly. The time consumed by work becomes almost thirty-nine per cent of the total weekly available waking hours, while mobile and/or social media consumption is almost sixteen per cent of total weekly waking hours, with eating, drinking, and house activities forming a little above eight per cent of total weekly waking hours. What is your dashboard telling you; what are your time ratios for working on your dreams and goals? How do you know where you are going and how are you going to get there without gauging your efforts.

This is not time management – It's Effort Management

What is the difference between time management and effort management? The first tries to control time by stuffing it with tasks; the second is about channelling effort within time in both amount and repetition while considering the significance of that effort on the overall time available. It is designed to help determine how we are using the only two resources that we have: time and ourselves. It helps us to understand where the results are coming from, and which activities provide us with more information for better decision-making.

The challenge always remains; we often take on new initiatives without appropriate arrangements. We assume we have sufficient time to accommodate the task. We believe we can do it, but as we squeeze the tasks in, something else must give way. Our habits push us back to the same old cycle.

Something must change to accommodate the new initiative. That change is decided by how serious you are about this new thing, and how often and how long it is going to take to get it. We make changes without looking at our current information. We add new goals in without full awareness of where the time is coming from to achieve such goals. How do you know if you are going to get what you are after if you are not tracking your progress? How will you know when a project will be completed to the level of quality you are seeking through the time and effort you put in? This applies to your life project as well as any other project.

Self-deception

Now that you know how to read your numbers, it is time to put it to work if you want to see improved achievements. We have a way of fooling our inner minds to believe that we are more successful or have achieved more than we really have. Dr Robert Trivers says, 'Keeping true record is the only way to eliminate self-deception. Knowing the truth about yourself might not be easy to deal with, but it's the simplest way to success.'

Don't be quick to dismiss the idea of recording and tracking what you do-in-time. People do what feels good in the short term, while it can hurt them eventually. People are selfish by nature and tend to block things that do not agree with their feelings. We are also illogical at times. We love to think that we are logical, but the fact is that we are not. Some of us are more rational than others, even phenomenally successful people. The elite are obsessed to the point that it is not rational; their decisions can appear illogical to most of us. But when they do things that the average person does not do, we admire them and praise them, not because of what they did but because of the results they achieved; results forgive the elite, and we praise how they are and what they do. People cannot function socially without labels, which help us to understand the world as we know it. *We need labels to compartmentalise the information we constantly collect. Those labels are called self-organising; they are how we accept or dismiss information and people.* This is how the human brain works.

For years, Greg Duval, a former high-school quarterback, kept adding pounds while telling himself he just needed to go for a run to take off the extra weight, finding every excuse to put off exercise. The rationale he used helped him feel as though he was in control. Recently, he approached fifty years of age and took an inventory of what he did in time. This is when he realised he was deceiving himself. He was lying to himself about how much he ate and how much he exercised.

It takes strong self-awareness to keep self-deception from becoming a hindrance in life, jobs, or relationships. Keeping a record of what you do-in-time provides self-awareness that leads to self-discipline. It will stop you from deceiving yourself. It will be your truth, your foundation, the cornerstone to building a successful life. It is worth noting that self-deception is not just lying or faking our thoughts and feelings. It can be deeper than that. It involves psychological forces that keep us from acknowledging a threatening truth about ourselves, says Delroy Paulhus, a psychology professor at the University of British Columbia.

The good feeling mechanism that comes from the excuses we produce to counter bad feelings and failures is what is stopping you – it is you. You are the captain of your journey; you are also the time-waster. You are the only mechanic that can fix your life vessel. People you allow to board your life vessel will either help and support you or become dead weight, dragging your vessel down and preventing it from moving up and forward. Choose your company carefully. They are the tipping point in your journey. No one should travel alone and choosing your travel partner is as important as figuring out your destination.

Doing the same routine every week will not change your ratios. What changes your ratio is a shift in what you do-in-time. The idea behind time ratios is not to change your entire lifestyle or to be something that you are not. Instead, the idea is to put on your dashboard activities that have to do with achieving your goals. Monitoring your efforts is the pathway to results; it helps to fit your new efforts into your normal life. It does not require changes to your personal psychology or your entire life. Changes are to be implemented as smoothly and easily as possible by looking at your entire time landscape filled in the best possible places. Time ratios are not about doing more with less time or creating what is not. They are about working towards long-term results while feeling good in the interim and eliminating bad feelings by relying on facts and realities.

Let's say that you want to be an excellent swimmer; to be so, you must practise. Deciding on how much you practise depends on what level of excellence you are aiming for and how quickly you want to get there, and both are related to your personal capabilities. The higher the level you want to reach, the more practice is needed. The sooner you want to get there, the more practice you have to do with more repetition. When you give yourself more time to be excellent, your schedule can be more relaxed. Let's assume that with your current personal capabilities, you would like to reach a local level of competition in swimming. From research, we have concluded that a starting swimmer needs about two thousand hours of practice to reach that level of competition; to reach that level within two years means that you must train for one thousand hours per year on average, which means around twenty hours of training every week for fifty-two weeks in the year.

Twenty hours of swimming practice every week is around twelve per cent of your total available weekly time or more than 17.4 per cent of your waking hours. Your time ratio for swimming practice needs to be 17.4 per cent every week to achieve your goal within two years. A time ratio of less than 17.4 per cent per week for training means it will take longer to get to the level where you can win. If your time ratio required for training is consistently more than 17.4 per cent, it is safe to assume that you will be able to compete and win within two years or sooner with genuine effort. With genuine effort, you can be guaranteed that you will get to where you are going. Knowing your weekly time ratios will tell you for sure if you are on the right path or not. Time ratios should be your gauge for success.

The next question should be, 'Where do I get the 17.4 per cent from?' Looking at Table 7, time is fully consumed. You cannot get more time. You can only get the time needed from other activities. Some activities need to be reduced or replaced altogether. Having a goal is one thing; achieving it is another thing. To achieve such a goal means to do what it takes for as long as it takes to get it done. Time ratios tell us the whole story. The bigger the ratio, and the more persistence, the better the results.

The following chapters should provide more assistance in using time ratios, through the planning and designing of your do-in-time objectives, with simple tools for getting anything done while complementing your lifestyle, enjoying the ride, and having fun. The time ratio will be the best thing that has happened to you! It will give you the chance to immerse yourself in what you love the most while having positive effects on other parts of your life. It will give you a chance to balance your life and focus on what is important. What happens when your time ratio for a goal is running below its planned rate? Well, one of two things will happen. Either you will bring the time ratio to its required level as you go, or you will drop the goal. When you drop your goals, you then know for sure that your goals will not be achieved. You cannot say that you have a goal; you can only say that you have a wish. What happens when a goal-driven time ratio is below its planned level? It will tell you the kind of person you are – a doer or a dreamer.

CHAPTER 6

RESULTS FIRST

REVERSE-ENGINEER YOUR SUCCESS.

Working with engineers has taught me to always start from what it is we are trying to build. Starting with concept design, which is the target of the project once it is decided, we then move on to the detailed design of what exactly to build. Without having the result in mind first, no building or structure or project can be built. Then to design as built, which tells us how it is being built.

When you aim at nothing, you get nothing. Life is not the goal or the objective in itself; it is the journey towards achieving that objective that counts. In his book, *The 7 Habits of Highly Effective People,* Stephen Covey listed 'begin with the end in mind' as the second most important habit. Put simply, start from where you would like to be, as it will make it easier for you to reach your destination. It will give you the pathway to reach your destination. In addition, it can tell you if you are on the right path – or not.

Where purpose meets planning

This book is not trying to answer the question of the purpose of life; that is for you to figure out. *A target in mind does not answer the life purpose questions, though it can serve the purpose of life very well through getting goals done.* Starting at the end in this context is for those goals with the ultimate purpose to be served. As a concept, it works for all goals and objectives to be achieved.

The time ratios deal with more of the how and not the what, when it comes to goal achievement.

Should your life have a purpose? Only you can answer that. Ask yourself, what is life without purpose? It is an empty and hollow life. It is not unusual for people to live without a grand purpose – their purpose is simply to live. A lack of insight into yourself may lead to lingering feelings of emptiness, depression, anxiety and resentment, guilt, and shame – some call it bad luck. Feeling empty is a symptom of borderline personality dis-order. Life-turning moments ascend from a clear purpose. Life without a purpose is a lost life in the sea of humanity. Which road should you take if you do not know your destination? Are you doing good or bad? Are you succeeding or failing? How do you measure your life and your self-worth?

The sad fact is, with or without a purpose, moments will be consumed regardless of what you do.

Three types of people

My thirty-something years of experience have shown me three types of people in this world. The first type is someone who has an unclouded vision of their purpose in life with clear goals to achieve. It doesn't matter if they started with a purpose or not, or if their purpose evolved to be where it is now; it feels like they were born with it. Once they have it, they have it, and they go for it. Not getting it done is not an option for this type of person. Once that purpose in their life is clear, working towards it forms an integral part of their character. It defines who they are and makes them feel as though they were made for that purpose.

Some of them have outrageous, unbelievable, or even unrealistic goals. At the start, they might be called crazy, with not so many believing in them. Others may mock them and laugh at them until they reach their objectives. Once it's done, everyone wants to be their friend, to be part of their story, part of their success. Those achievers will reach new heights, places no person has reached before. They change history or, better yet, they make history. They are in every generation from the beginning and will be around to the end. They do not care what others have to say about them. They are positive and obsessive. It is hard to distinguish between them and their purpose in life.

The second type is someone who installs goals into their life. They have a clear distinction between life goals and life purpose, They have different goals at different life stages. They have multiple goals: career, family, personal and health. They are not defined by their goals but by their life purpose. Most succeed, and some fail. Often, failure occurs because they use techniques and tools that do not work. Some keep at it; others get frustrated, distracted, or derailed by situations and circumstances, and a few completely drop it. Those who keep at it have successful careers. They have good homes with good families. They are more balanced than the first type, and they are top-tier achievers, successful entrepreneurs, and career leaders.

They are positive individuals. They like to be around positive, successful people. They seek to learn and do better. They work on sharpening their skills. They might get knocked down, but they get back up. They believe in themselves. They trust their own capabilities, and they do not believe that success is based on luck. Rather, they are all about work and effort. They are persistent, consistent, and disciplined. They make things happen.

The third type is someone who has no goals or purpose and is just floating in time. Days come and go, in much the same way – as routine. They keep moving, and life keeps moving as they live in it. They have jobs, and families, though I am not sure how happy they are. While they are content, most are excuse-makers, whiners, and blamers; they believe that they are not lucky and that the other guys are luckier. They are busy but have nothing to show for it. They have what life has given to them. Life is what happens to them – no actions but reactions.

Ask yourself...

Which type are you? If you are seeking the true answer, look at your actions and what you are doing. Do you have a purpose, goals, objectives, or things that you want to achieve? Then ask yourself the important question of how much you do-in-time to serve those purposes, goals, and/or objectives. Are you taking responsibility for your actions, or are you blaming everything else or making excuses for not getting your goals done? Can you recognise that you are where you are because of your own actions? Are you taking charge of your life by doing all it takes to serve your purpose? Are your efforts genuine, or are you floating? Are you throwing your time away? Do your habits run your time or does your time decide your habits? Are you watching your dashboard? Are you in command of your journey, or do you feel hopeless? Only you can answer these questions. The answers will tell you what type of person you are.

So, you are the type of guy who has goals you want to work on. You are motivated. You want to lose that extra weight. You want financial freedom. You want to be a good parent by spending more time with your family. You want to be doing what you love the most. That is all great! But life as we know it can be overwhelming, which can lead to doing nothing. The most effective way to deal with life goals is to have short-, medium-, and long-term goals. The number of goals must be reasonable within periods of time until some goals are completed. Then new goals can be added, or some goals can be replaced, as life is not constant. Having too many goals is a distraction that is overwhelming and counterproductive. It is an obstacle rather than a help.

A professor of business at Columbia University Business School and a leading researcher on choice, Sheena Iyengar, suggests that the magical number of choices is around seven. She confirms that having fewer choices and fewer options empowers us to make stronger and more satisfying choices. On the other hand, in his book *18 Minutes*, Peter Bregman reached a different magic number of things to focus on and work on in one year after a tremendous amount of trial and error. That number of goals is five. From my thirty years of experience in multiple industries across the globe, I tend to agree with Professor Iyengar, more so than Bregman. I believe that seven is a better number of goals to work on and/or things to focus on in a year, but the choice is yours. Those seven things can be goals for more than a year; they can be goals for any length of time that works for you based on the nature of those goals.

How many goals?

The number of goals and objectives that you choose is not crucial, so long as it is not going to overwhelm or impede you. Nor does it matter if you select goals for less than a year, for one, three, five or more years. The length of time is up to you. Your total set of goals at one time is suggested not to be more than nine or less than three – your magic number should be in between. It is advised that you divide your goals into categories, and you can have smaller goals inside your bigger goals in each category. For instance, categories can be personal, business-related, professional, religious, or spiritual. Your family can be a category. You choose what works for you. Choose what goals you intend to reach go into each category. Select your categories based on your aspirations, dreams, and purpose. Your target should be around seven goals in all the categories at any given time. Study after study shows that having many goals to work on is overwhelming to the point that none of the goals is worked on – too many choices lead to no choice.

This is a framework for the number of goals to have at one time. It should serve your purpose better if you have at least one long-term goal that extends for more than five years. A goal with enough to do-in-time should make you great, an expert, an elite of that category; sufficient doing-in-time is what it takes to become the champion.

High achievers

In his hugely popular book, *Outliers*, Malcolm Gladwell used research published by Anders Ericsson in 1993 to develop his argument. Ericsson was a Professor at the University of Colorado who published a book called *The Role of Deliberate Practice in the Acquisition of Expert Performance*. In this, he explains that to be a true expert, you need on average ten thousand hours of practice; to be excellent, you need around eight thousand hours of practice, and to be above average, you will need around four thousand hours of practice in that subject. Some responded to this theory by saying that you must be talented as well to reach the level of an elite performer over ten thousand hours and that the expert level cannot happen without talent. They may be right, but what will happen if you are not talented, and you don't practise – what would you have?

Showing up is important, but it cannot be mistaken for doing. Going to work for more than eight hours a day, five days a week or more, every week of the year does not make you an expert unless you are learning and doing new things at work.

Working my way up to organisational leadership roles around the globe for more than three decades, watching people working through the ranks – as individuals or in teams, as employees, contractors, or competitors, customers, and bosses, of different cultures, backgrounds, education, ethnicity, or belief systems – has cemented in me the notion that *success exists as a simple equation:* **genuine effort over time.**

The more genuine effort you put in for longer periods of time, the more you will achieve. For a few people, putting in a genuine effort is what they do all the time. Those individuals are champions, gold medallists, prize winners, runners-up, and iconic people in business, sports, music, arts, and other areas. They are the elite.

But what happens if you do not want to be a champion, gold medallist, or icon? What if all you want is to achieve your goals and objectives? Is that considered to be unsuccessful? The short answer is no. You are successful when you achieve what you want. If your goal is to have a more balanced life and more family time, then success is measured by achieving that goal. Success is getting what you set as your goal in life. It is about fulfilling your purpose in life, whatever that may be.

It was a life-changing period going to college with most of my high-school friends. In the first few semesters, I struggled with most of my subjects. The more classes I took, the worse my grades got and the more depressed and frustrated I became. Things got worse for me, and that was when I discovered that my high-school friends' grades were good. They were doing okay in college, but I was not. I felt like a total failure. With a final warning for academic performance, things got even worse. I had only two options – either bring my grades up quickly or get kicked out of college. In the following semester, I took easy classes in a desperate push to bring my grades up. One class, Economics 101, led to a series of events. Looking back at that point in time, it was a turning point in my life. The professor, Dr Akram Baqaeen, made the class incredibly fun and enjoyable. He engaged all the students, and his office door was open all the time for students seeking help, and I was. I needed someone to talk to; he listened patiently, guided me through as much as he could, and then sent me to the student affairs counsellor. What I remember, without a doubt, is the guidance I received from my counsellor, Ms Haya Dawany. She showed me how to compare myself to a younger me. She showed me that the most important win is when I win against myself. The hardest struggle is against ourselves, and success is when you win that struggle. I discovered that the only rival that I needed to beat is in me. I got my grades up, and I graduated from college. I owe both Dr Akram Baqaeen and Haya Dawany a great deal of gratitude.

Success is not competing against others. It is to compete against all things that are trying to stop you from achieving your goals. I measure success one goal at a time. Success is when we recognise that previous efforts have not achieved our goals and that we need to work more to improve those efforts. Success is knowing that what we do-in-time is what it takes to make something happen.

The target is to get to where you plan to go, which takes quality effort done in time. Working your time Ratio of Success is your dashboard – regardless of where you are going; your speed is what works for you. You decide – fast or slow. It's up to you, so long as you know that faster means higher time ratios, and slower means lower time ratios.

Goals and Time Ratios

If we work with the concepts presented in Anders Ericsson's *The Role of Deliberate Practice in the Acquisition of Expert Performance*, then we can expect something like this: work your time ratios backward based on the length of your plan. For example, if your plan's aim is for you to become a subject expert in five years, then you need eight hours a day, five days a week, all year long to be excellent. Six hours a day, five days a week, all year long will place you in the good category, while three hours a day, five days a week, all year long will put you in the average category on a five-year plan. Table 8 shows the ratios needed for each level of expertise based on a five-year plan.

Five Year Plan to Become an Expert	All week Hours (168)	Week hours excluding sleep time (112)
Expertise Level	**Time Ratio Needed**	**Time Ratio Needed**
Top Category	23.8%	35.7%
Good Category	17.9%	26.8%
Average Category	8.9%	13.4%

TABLE 8. EXAMPLE OF WEEKLY ALLOTMENT OF TIME

It is important to note that flexibility is necessary when working on your target. Not all types of goals require the same amount of time ratio. Different goals have different effort requirements, though the principle is the same. How to do it:

Step 1: select your goals

Keep it simple. Start with categories within your life that you enjoy working on. Write those categories on a sheet of paper, and keep those categories to a maximum of three. It is okay if there are more, but it is not advised. Now, write under each category the goals you want to achieve. This is not a wish list. You should only include goals that you want and are ready to pursue on a regular basis. It is recommended to keep goals between two and three in each category. Goals can be adjusted, replaced, or eliminated as they are achieved, and new goals can be added with time. Select goals that you really want to achieve. The shorter the list, the better. Divide your goals into smaller and more defined goals in each category – for example, Family category, Business or Professional category, and Personal category – with one to three goals in each. You should be clear about your goals and how they are going to work with your overall weekly do-in-time.

Step 2: decide what level you want to reach

Decide on which level of achievement you want to get to. Remember, the higher the level, the more time and repetition are required on that activity to achieve such a level. In addition, a higher level of achievement requires a higher level of quality effort.

The time ratio is built around the level/s at which you set your goal. If your goal is to lose twenty kilograms within three months, this requires greater effort than losing the same in six months or losing five kilograms within three months. The time ratio for exercise will be different for each. The same principle applies to other goals. How good of a pianist you would like to be is what decides your music practice ratio. Do you want to pass an exam? How much of your time is set aside for study? You can try it with anything. Start with the level you want to achieve and the length of time in which you want to achieve it.

Before starting this book, I estimated that it would take around one hundred sixty to one hundred eighty hours of effort to get it done. This meant four hours a week for around forty to forty-five weeks. If I missed a week worth of work, then I needed to double up the week after to keep to my goal. Four hours a week is about 3.5 per cent of my available weekly time. This was my time ratio for every week to get it done as planned. My weekly dashboard would tell me if I was on target or not with my weekly time ratios as I tracked my do-in-time activities. It did not mean I could not make the targeted schedule shorter by increasing the weekly time ratio dedicated to authoring this book.

Step 3: decide on your effort's quality

You have decided on your goals and selected the level of achievement that you would like to reach for each goal. What type of effort is needed to achieve each goal or what is the quality of effort needed? Starting at the end of what you want to achieve means having a vision, a picture of what the result/s should look like. This is a sure way of not getting lost. Starting with the end in mind is starting with an image of the destination; it is a picture of what the end looks like. It allows different options to get there to become clearer, which allows for different choices on how to get it done. It displays the possibilities of what is required to get it done.

Step 4: track your time ratios

Tracking your weekly time ratio provides your dashboard with the necessary information about the effort required in amount and frequency. It provides a guarantee that you are going to the correct destination at the desired speed. It should put your mind at ease. Your dashboard adds value and meaning to your life journey. It is your needle to the north.

This is an opportunity to work on your purpose, a calling if you choose it to be. Having clear categories with clear goals set in them will make it easier to answer such a calling. Do not be afraid and follow your heart but take your brain with you. As once stated by Steve Jobs, 'Your time is limited, so do not waste it living someone else's life… Do not be trapped by dogma, which is living with the results of other people's expectations. Do not let the noise of others' opinions mask your own inner voice. And most important, have the courage to follow your heart and intuition.'

Saying no is more important than saying yes. Say no to time-suckers. Say no to things that consume your time without inching you forward. It is time to get unbusy.

CHAPTER 7

Let us get unbusy

Keep, enhance, and remove.

"The way we spend our time defines who we are."

— Jonathan Estrin

Kids, family, career, friends, health, passion, entertainment, making money, sports, events, relaxing, travelling, shows, movies, education, training, and the internet. So much to do, so many interesting people to meet, dreams to chase, goals to achieve, and a purpose to serve. Life is full of opportunities, activities, people we care about, and causes we want to pursue. We want meaning in our lives. We spend a great portion of our lives chasing meaning without ever stumbling upon it. We are so busy, we do not have time anymore for anything else. We submit to a multitude of things that compete to consume our time.

In a study published in the *Harvard Business Review* in April 2019, the author explains how people claim they are busy and asks if they are truly busy in a productive way. David Rock, the author of *Brain at Work*, found that people are not focused on work for longer than six hours within a forty-hour work week. This gives us a good feeling of acting, sounding busy and looking busy. It gives us a sense of importance. It helps to assure us of our self-worth, while the truth is we are not at all productive. This is called 'fake work'. Are you busy with true or fake work?

The answer is simple. Real work is aligned with goals and objectives; it has true results. Fake work gets you nowhere. You can be remarkably busy with no significant result. Being busy is not a goal. Adding more to your daily schedule is not always the solution. We confuse motion for action. We do not intend to perform fake work. We do it because it is easy. It is less painful to convince ourselves that we are working hard, and that by working hard, we have no time, we are in demand, and we are important, which is not true. No one wants to do fake work. When we do not stop to think about what we are doing and why we are doing it, it gets easier for fake work to sneak up into our daily routines. It's comforting; it gives a bit of meaning. Over time, I discovered that knowing the difference between true and fake work is not a random act. It requires deliberate actions to separate fake from true work. One relatively effortless way to do this is by tracking what you do-in-time and if such actions are serving your goals and objectives. It is to track effort and the results. Time schedules tell only part of the story. It is a snapshot with no clear connection to results and is not necessarily serving your goals and objectives.

Time to clear the clutter

We are not making it easier to get things done. We are allowing useless activities to take over our time, and we are spending more time than ever on the internet, particularly on social media. According to brandsearchgroup.com, time spent on social media has increased to one hundred fifty-four minutes per day on average over the past year in comparison to sixty minutes per day in 2012. That is more than a two hundred fifty per cent increase in ten years. That is one hundred fifty-four minutes of fake-busy added to our daily lives. The amount of time we spend on social media also affects how we feel and act.

Our time is becoming more cluttered with greater distractions and time-sucking activities. Tech companies, commercial enterprises, and entertainers are competing for our attention, wanting us to consume what they are selling, not only with a financial cost but also at the cost of time, which is more precious. In addition, the way we are consuming content and data has created new types of stress and anxiety without giving us a clear destination.

Taking a step back from our daily lives is a good starting point. It helps us clean our time from clutter. By tracking and doing what counts, time ratios will set the record straight on what needs to get done and what needs to be dumped based on goals and objectives. Time-wasters have no place in successful people's timesheets. If it does not serve a goal, it needs to go. Time ratios will lead to dumping things much faster than adding things to what to do-in-time.

Tracking time ratios is a simple tool, which has a powerful effect on your success. It tells the story of what you do with your time. It separates true from fake. It keeps efforts laser-focused on goals. It warns you when you are off track. Table 9a has activities listed randomly, while Table 9b has the same activities categorised in highlighted colours. Organising activities by categories and grouping each activity under the proper category makes the dashboard easier to read and more efficient to manage. Being prepared is more than half of the winning, and having work done at the start is being prepared.

Activities	Total Minutes Used	Total Hours Used
Sleep	3150	52.50
shower/ dress	220	3.67
breakfast	150	2.50
News & updates	225	3.75
commute to	315	5.25
work	2680	44.67
commute back	325	5.42
Eat & drink	290	4.83
Relax -family	175	2.92
Mobile - social media	1100	18.33
Personal Care	165	2.75
TV & Internet	375	6.25
GYM & Sports	180	3.00
Personal Development	195	3.25
House activities	285	4.75
Travel	0	-
friends & Entertainment	250	4.17
Total	**10080**	**168**

TABLE 9A. ACTIVITIES RANDOMLY LISTED

Activities	Total Minutes Used	Total Hours Used
Sleep	3,150	52.50
shower/ dress	220	3.67
GYM & Sports	180	3.00
Travel	-	-
breakfast	150	2.50
Eat & drink	290	4.83
commute to	315	5.25
work	2,680	44.67
commute back	325	5.42
Relax -family	175	2.92
House activities	285	4.75
Personal Care	165	2.75
Personal Development	195	3.25
friends & Entertainment	250	4.17
News & updates	225	3.75
Mobile - Social Media	1,100	18.33
TV & Internet	375	6.25
Total	**10,080**	**168**

TABLE 9B. ACTIVITIES GROUPED (AND COLOURED) ACCORDING TO CATEGORY

The categories in Table 9b are divided into three distinct sections. The first section is underlined with a thickened black line, the second section is between the black line and the red line, and the third and concluding section is below the red line.

The first section is the 'keep' section, a 'must have' section that includes fixed activities that are daily, while the time used might be different. These activities are essential for any person and include things such as sleep, family time, house activities, eating and drinking, and physical activities. These activities are set in stone. For example, changing your commuting time to and from work requires a change of work or home location. It can be done, but that is a big step that doesn't happen often.

The second section is the 'enhanced' section. This involves the 'sense of belonging' activities that can be negotiated, which does not mean 'not doing'. What it means is that those activities can be grouped into various categories or moved around. For example, 'personal care' can be part of different activities such as relaxing or sports activities.

The third section is the 'remove' section; it includes aspirations or activities that can be eliminated or reconfigured to a minimum level.

A 'must-have' section includes things like rest, food, security, and money for your needs. The 'sense of belonging' section includes things like family and friends. The 'aspiration' section includes things that you aspire to achieve: your goals and purpose. This is not suggesting that the first and second sections are without goals; they are. But the time to reach such goals should come from the last section. Understanding the nature of 'must-have' activities is critical. Life cannot proceed without needs -- a foundation to achieve a more active and fulfilling life.

After creating your list, view your sections, categories, and activities in each, and consider the time consumed in these sections. Spending five hours a day on the internet watching shows and social media will take away from your life without you realising it. Saying no to activities in the third section is more important than saying yes to a new project; you need space for new projects. Say no to too many hours on the internet, say no to binging on television shows, and say no to activities that do not serve your goals and objectives. Say no to unimportant or non-urgent matters with better planning by focusing on what is important.

How you work on enhancing sections is determined by your goals and objectives. In the example above, the internet and social media are included in a section that should be removed. This doesn't apply if social media is the way you make your living, or if it is your job. The elimination or reduction should be based on your situation and only come from you. You will know time-wasters once they are identified by you. Put them at the bottom of your dashboard, and put the 'must have', which cannot change, at the top of your dashboard. Put 'can change' in the middle of the dashboard and what you 'should change' at the bottom of the list.

Once you make space in time by removing time-wasters, you should add new activities based on your new goals and objectives. The process of self-discovery will help you select how hard or how soft your time cuts into your activities. It does not have to be an absolute cut. You don't have to stop using the internet or social media, for example, but they shouldn't be used to the same degree. You should say no to six hours of internet use per day, and yes to two hours instead. This is to get unbusy, not to stop your life. Don't go hard with time cuts. It will not work. But do not fool yourself either by making insignificant changes. If you do not do the work, the job will not get done.

Table 10 is an example of the time change in the last two sections. Section two is reduced by a small amount of time on a weekly basis while the third section is reduced by larger chunks of time. The totals in the end column will show the impact on weekly time.

Activities	Total Minutes Used	Total Minutes Reduced	Total New Minutes	Total New Hours
Sleep	3,150	-	3,150.00	52.50
shower/ dress	220	-	220.00	3.67
GYM & Sports	180	-	180.00	3.00
Travel	-	-	-	-
breakfast	150	-	150.00	2.50
Eat & drink	290	-	290.00	4.83
commute to	315	-	315.00	5.25
work	2,680	-	2,680.00	44.67
commute back	325	-	325.00	5.42
Relax -family	175	-	175.00	2.92
House activities	285	-	285.00	4.75
Personal Care	165	30.00	135.00	2.25
Personal Development	195	30.00	165.00	2.75
friends & Entertainment	250	60.00	190.00	3.17
News & updates	225	120.00	105.00	1.75
Mobile - Social Media	1,100	900.00	200.00	3.33
TV & Internet	375	300.00	75.00	1.25
Total	**10,080**	**1,440**	**8,640.00**	**144.00**

TABLE 10. WEEKLY ACTIVITIES WITH ENHANCED AND
REDUCED TIME ALLOTMENTS (IN MINUTES) IN SECTIONS TWO AND THREE

Note that in Table 10, the maximum reduction comes from mobile phone use, social media, TV, and other internet activities. The total time reduced is twenty-four hours per week, which is almost five hours a day, five days a week, every week. Imagine what could be accomplished with twenty-four hours of time a week. With that much time available, you can and should conquer the world. Further enhancement of what you do-in-time can continue as you go forward. Do not do too much at the start. Do not overcut or over-enhance your time ratios suddenly. Do it as comfortably as possible, and do not overwhelm yourself – that is a push for failure. Make changes that align with the way you are and who you are. This is a tool to navigate your direction to success. It is a headlight into the darkness of fake-busy, time-wasters and self-deception.

Hard choices, good choices

Success happens by design, not by chance, and such design stems from actions decided by choice. Steve Jobs once said, 'My favourite things in life do not cost any money. The most precious resource we all have is time.' He realised, just like many others, that time is the most undervalued resource we have, equal in distribution but not in length. We deal with time like it will go on without an end.

No one should be judged based on how many years they spent on Earth but rather on what she/he did in time. That should be the true judgement.

Getting unbusy and saying no to time-wasting habits in daily life is a challenge – this concept is not for average people. It is where hard choices and tough actions are made. Facing your busyness with the truth of your daily actions is easy if you choose to do so with full disclosure and honesty with yourself. No one else will do this for you. It is your time. It will be your results. And you will be the judge. From Table 10, twenty-four hours of time per week can reform your life in so many positive ways. That time, when aligned with your goals, can only lead to a successful and prosperous life. Table 11 shows an example of what can be done in twenty-four hours per week. You can learn to be a good guitarist, author a book, and get an MBA, if not more. You can do many more things. Or you can direct more time to other activities for greater impact. In return, what did you lose? Nothing! You have gained much more than you think.

Research published by Child Mind Institute exhibited that there is indeed a correlation between spending copious amounts of time on social media platforms and depression. It can fuel the feeling of emptiness. In addition, some of the accounts on social media can impact the way you feel about yourself as the people running them look and sound much better and more successful than you, which can lead to depression and anxiety. In an article by Caroline Miller published at the Child Mind Institute, she noted that: 'In several studies, teenage and young adult users who spend the most time on Instagram, Facebook and other platforms were shown to have a higher rate of reported depression than those who spent the least amount of time.'

Activities	Total Minutes Used	Total Minutes Reduced	Total New Minutes	Total New Hours
Sleep	3,150	-	3,150.00	52.50
shower/ dress	220	-	220.00	3.67
GYM & Sports	180	-	180.00	3.00
Travel	-	-	-	-
breakfast	150	-	150.00	2.50
Eat & drink	290	-	290.00	4.83
commute to	315	-	315.00	5.25
work	2,680	-	2,680.00	44.67
commute back	325	-	325.00	5.42
Relax -family	175	-	175.00	2.92
House activities	285	-	285.00	4.75
Personal Care	165	30.00	135.00	2.25
Personal Development	195	30.00	165.00	2.75
Photography			300.00	5.00
Write a book			240.00	4.00
Get an MBA			900.00	15.00
friends & Entertainment	250	60.00	190.00	3.17
News & updates	225	120.00	105.00	1.75
Mobile - Social Media	1,100	900.00	200.00	3.33
TV & Internet	375	300.00	75.00	1.25
Total		1,440	10,080.00	168.00

TABLE 11. WEEKLY ACTIVITIES WITH A RE-ALIGNMENT

For some of us, to believe that we are busy is to believe that we are important and in demand. This is a self-prophecy to keep ourselves occupied with all sorts of things, and now more than ever, with mobile phones and tablets, we spend more time playing online games, flipping through social media apps one after another, and getting hooked. We immerse ourselves in images and videos because it feels good. We are entertained. We have to say no to ourselves before we say it to anyone or anything else. Warren Buffett once said, 'Successful people say no to almost everything.' Saying no, getting unbusy, is challenging. It is a struggle with yourself and your feelings as it is easier to fake busy.

In today's world, high-tech advances, social media proliferation, internet e-commerce and home delivery, income growth, inflation, and political and cultural changes all add to the changes in the use of our time. We cannot keep up. It is not a race anymore; it is a chase. We are no longer racing one another; we are chasing things. We are chasing every moment to use online and chasing social demands online, which is something we did not have before. We are chasing financial demands that are growing by the day and chasing to cope with political and social changes all around us. There is so much going on, we are offered an unlimited number of choices for what to do with our time. However, choices can hinder our ability to decide, and we end up doing nothing. This is where less is more.

In a study led by Sheena Iyengar, a research assistant presented one group of customers with six different flavours of jam in a supermarket, while twenty-four different flavours of jam were presented to another group of customers. The study showed that the group presented with twenty-four flavours of jam were overly excited at the sampling table but bought almost nothing. The group that was presented with six flavours bought a jam like the one they sampled by the time they finished shopping. The group with fewer choices had effectively engaged much more in the process, tenfold, than the group with more choices. It is time to unload daily schedules from so much to do-in-time to achieve better quality results.

What to say no should not be random. It should not be selected on beliefs but facts. Saying no to idle time with nothing to do is the first step towards success, but it is not the full story. Saying no is just the beginning of your time-ratio change. It is a must-do adjustment, replacing time-wasting activities with activities that serve your success.

Having a purpose to work for is an enticing prospect that explains the why, which will lead the way to how it should get done. Some people call it the destination. Others call it the 'vision'. Regardless of the name, you need to have a picture of what the result/s should look like. With that, you can plan the road, the pathway, to those results. If you cannot plan the pathway by yourself, then research how to get it done. For example, if you are thinking about getting your MBA but do not know how many credits it will take or how many hours you need to allocate for studying, consult graduate schools or education programs. They will provide you with all the details. Then you can work that into your time ratios. If you want to be a good pianist, your instructor will let you know how many hours it might take after assessing your skills. Do the research. It can be part of your time ratios for a few weeks until you are done. That task is your initial phase of planning. Choose your research based on defined goals and objectives.

Time ratios at work

Time ratios focus on measuring where your efforts are expended. Simply ask if those weekly do-in-time efforts are performed as planned to achieve success, one week at a time, one task at a time. If not completed, they can be shifted, if this does not become a habit. Keeping a daily time inventory of activities is mandatory for the overall success of your plan. You cannot afford to lose track of monitoring activities. If it happens that one entry is missed, do that activity when you remember, immediately. Do not ignore it. If the recording is done accurately, you will not be controlled; you will be in control.

Starting with what it is you want to get done will provide information to design the pathway to that goal. It will help to decide what kind of efforts are needed and for how long. The repetition, quality, and length of such efforts are the three milestones that you should install on the dashboard for measuring and re-measuring. Effort versus results: the right amount, type, and repetition of effort will lead to the right results, which is a success. Plans are good, but planning is everything. It requires us to slow down at every turn and check if we are still heading in the right direction. The dashboard is insurance against distractions, derailed efforts, and procrastination.

CHAPTER 8

DESIGN YOUR PATHWAY TO SUCCESS

PLANNING IS EVERYTHING.

"Plans are nothing; planning is everything."

— Dwight Eisenhower

Imagine this scenario. You put in your mind that you want to achieve a particular goal. It excites you. In the beginning, you are incredibly determined to make it happen. A few weeks later, or at best, a few months later, you are back to the same old ways, and the plan is no longer in action.

In an article by Inc.com, it was stated that approximately eighty per cent of people who make New Year's resolutions drop them by the second week of February. The good news is that it is normal to give up on your plans; the shocking news is we do it without actual realisation.

One reason people do not stick to their plans for more than six weeks is a lack of planning and monitoring. In addition to this, we hate change. While having a plan is great, plans only deal with what it is we want to get done. Planning, on the other hand, deals with how to get it done. In execution, the how is as critical for success as the what. In the previous chapters, we covered different methods and tools such as monitoring at the end of each day, goals and activities categories, the difference between those categories based on necessity and objectives, and what activities need to be reduced, cancelled, or added. This chapter will cover the way you design the activities that will form your Ratio of Success.

Genuine efforts

Planning is a process that demands a detailed exploration of the options, mitigation risks, and contingencies, which is required when plans get off track. *Mike Tyson said, 'Everybody has a plan until they get hit for the first time.'*

At the first obstacle, most people fold. Some put up a bit of resistance; however, most give up. Knowing what to expect and what resources you have will help in selecting the proper structure for what to do, how to do it, and when to do it. And this will lead to getting bigger goals done. People give up because they have not broken down, step by step, the requirements, possibilities, alternative options, and challenges that are involved. Going on a road trip to X town is the plan. Planning is selecting when to do it, how to do it, which mode of transportation to use, and if you are going to drive yourself, what vehicle to use, and deciding whether it is ready, if it has enough fuel for the trip, who will go with you, which road to take, how long it will take, what happens if there is a traffic jam, and so on. These are the types of issues that planning deals with: finding the answers, alternatives, and possibilities to ensure the completion of the job.

Back in the days when I was working for Outsource International, a multinational staffing company in the United States, I had earned a promotion to the position of regional director. I was given the opportunity to start a new office in Greenville, South Carolina. With a fresh promotion and a new office in unfamiliar territory, my first task was to get the office off the ground by generating revenue in that market. The business plans for the new office were completed by a corporate team. The plans suggested that revenues should start within two months of the office opening. For the first three months, the sales team generated zero revenue. Another three months went by, and sales remained at zero. The business plans and feasibility studies suggested that sales should have started long ago by this point, and I started doubting myself and my team. Our sales team started doubting the plans – it was a national staffing company that had been operating for more than thirty years with more than one hundred offices across the nation. Our business was proven, yet we were not getting any sales in Greenville. We did not know what we were doing wrong; we didn't know what the exact problem was.

We believed that someone had made a mistake in the business plan, and frustrated, self-doubting, and ready to give up, we asked for help from corporate. They sent one guy, who worked directly with our sales team. After a few visits to potential customers, it was clear that no one from corporate talked to any potential customers while doing the business plan. Assumptions were made that Greenville was just like any other market in the country, which was not true; customers in Greenville, South Carolina, had long-binding contracts with staffing suppliers due to local market conditions such as fierce competition among suppliers, lack of resources available, and competition among customers for those resources. Greenville had one of the highest number of staffing agencies in the country per capita. It also had the highest number of manufacturers per capita with not enough population to cover open jobs. Based on those numbers, business looked very promising for newcomers. No one from the corporate office had done any proper planning on how exactly revenue was going to be generated in this type of market. The studies assumed that Greenville was the same as all other markets. No strategy was in place, which meant that no clear action was to be implemented on the ground to deal with those new challenges. The corporate man made the necessary changes in the sales approach, offering an approach to match market conditions.

It took a long time to get the sales where they needed to be, and the cost for the company in time and money was much higher than budgeted for. If it hadn't had deep enough pockets, it could have been out of business. Do not assume that because you have a good business plan, it is going to work. It might not. Before corporate helped, I was ready to fold. I requested that the head office close the Greenville office on three separate occasions. Once the problem was identified, a new plan was advised, and within two years that same office was one of the highest-grossing revenue earners within the company.

How and how often

Designing your way to success starts with identifying your bigger goals and objectives of what you want to get done, and then deciding on what it will take to get it done. The first part is the what. The second part is the how. You should make your plans based on normal situations while allocating a small amount of time to deal with unexpected events and emergencies.

Your goals and decisions are based on your choices. Goals will not be of the same importance, relevance, length, and type, which impacts two critical matters in achieving your Ratio of Success: what effort is required in time, and how many times it needs to be done. These two matters are also influenced by personal capabilities, personal nature, and the surrounding environment. The bottom line is that results equal genuine effort over time. This is the *"equation of success"*.

We are all capable individuals and are all equal in the equation of success. We just need to figure out the length of time and frequency required to successfully complete our goals. It does not matter what type of person you are or where you come from. This equation applies to all of us in the same way. How much genuine effort you are prepared to do-in-time to achieve your goal and how many times you need to do the activity per week *(how long and how often)* to get it done is the difference as no two people are alike. The equation values will not be the same for any two individuals for the same exact goal. This is our uniqueness, like our fingerprints. While our goals can be the same and our routes to achieve those goals can be the same, the moments in each journey are never the same. What we do in those moments forms the differences among us.

Three-part equation

My son participated in a robotic competition in the United Kingdom. He wanted to win and asked me for advice. My advice to him recommended a hands-on approach. We started our work by focusing on the equation of success by breaking it down into its three parts: the desired result (first part), which for him was to win the competition; the time needed to build his robot (second part); and the genuine effort required (third part).

The genuine effort meant being true and honest in his research, preparation, teamwork, and execution. He started working with his teammate on the project, and at the end of each day, we sat down to review the time they had spent on the project and the quality of their efforts. Their efforts improved with every passing day. The team reviewed task distribution and task completion every day, and what we learned as individuals and as a group was that the quality of our efforts influenced the quality of our results. Allocating the proper number of hours with weekly frequency gave them the right amount of time to work on their ideas, solve problems, adjust to issues, and prepare.

The commitment to their own time ratios on the project guaranteed the project would be a successful one. My son and his team won first place in the competition, and from that day forward, he realised that genuine effort in time can, and will, deliver your goals to you. He went on to graduate with honours from high school and attend one of the best universities in the world for engineering. He also trained long enough to become a jujutsu champion. His sister and younger brother are also high achievers, and they understand that the quality of results is dictated by the quality of the efforts and time spent doing relevant activities my kids have become my mentors when it comes to genuine effort.

Another example is a college degree. The more courses you take per semester, the faster you will get your degree (given that you pass all your subjects). The more genuine effort you put into studying, the better your grades. You have a choice between allocating enough to do-in-time for college to graduate early, or you can look at your current ratios and design your pathway to a college degree based on that.

What stops us from applying the equation-of-success methods in our daily lives? For centuries, research has been conducted on human behaviours. You feel in control, and you are happy. It feels good, but when faced with the truth, it hurts. We cannot hurt ourselves, and we do not want to hurt ourselves, so what do we do? We make excuses. This allows us to go on with no pain, and no remorse. It provides justification that comes in handy and enables us to feel good about why we are not getting the job done, and life goes on.

Research has found that humans use excuses to feel good about themselves while not achieving their goals. Excuses are invented to alleviate the pain of confronting ourselves, of telling ourselves the truth about not getting something done because we have been lazy, chosen the easy way, or refused to face hard work. Admitting failure is painful, and we are not wired to tolerate pain. As shown by Pontari, Schlenker and Christopher in their research article 'Excuses and character: Identifying the problematic aspects of excuses.

When applying the equation of success, we should be working on things that are under our control, not things that are not under our control. What we can control in the equation of success is what we do-in-time and how genuine our efforts are. Our equation of success has to do with our individual goals, which can get tangled and intertwined with each other. They can overlap or connect, or they can depend on each other. They can be sequences, stacked, or bundled together. They are your goals; keep it simple.

Table 12 is an example of how to select categories with goals in each category. It also shows that goals are classified into short, medium, and long term, which is the cornerstone of designing your pathway to success. Time is only the first part of the three-part equation; this classification will help in allocating proper time ratios for each category. An integral part of the equation of success is the denominator of that equation.

Category	Goal	Short term	Medium term	Long term
Family	More time	More time	More time	More time
Personal	Lose weight	5 kg	10–15 kg	25 kg
	Photography	Amateur	Professional	Expert
Professional	Education		MBA	
	Change jobs	New job (more money)		

TABLE 12. GOAL SETTING IN SHORT-, MEDIUM-, AND LONG-TERM CATEGORIES

A goal that is listed in the short-, medium-, and long-term fields flourishes into a lifestyle. In Table 12, there is one new goal in the Family category, which is 'more' family time. This simple example is not to say how or in which way the extra time will be spent with family. It has the flexibility to be applied in the way that works for you. Your dashboard will tell you if it is happening or not. If not, you can adjust.

The short-, medium-, and long-term milestones should be based on self-discovery and the results decided by you. It is worth noting that all goals have constraints. For example, losing weight is constrained by your diet as well as your body type due to effort, which all require genuine efforts. If you are not getting the desired results, then examine your concept of 'genuine'. How genuine are your efforts? The answer should give you the proper answer you need to get it done.

The Personal category has two goals: to lose weight and to learn photography as a hobby. In the Professional category, there are two goals: one is short term, which is changing jobs, aiming for more money, and the other is medium term, which is getting an MBA. The time expected to get an MBA is around two years or longer; attaining an MBA degree as a goal has time constraints dictated by others. While changing jobs has constraints of its own – for example, market conditions, the demand for your specialisation, job availability, hiring managers, and others – what remains under your control is the genuine effort put into looking for a new job. While this is a short-term goal, it might have to be adjusted to a medium-term goal based on the situation you are in. Putting the goal in the right category is as important as selecting the goal itself. Any goal pursued in the wrong span of time has a negative impact.

You should consider a few things before you start to design your pathway to success using the equation of success. In Table 12, the Family category goal of more family time is in all three classes (i.e., the same goal was set for the short, medium, and long term). That is a lifestyle goal. Consider it as such while selecting and designing other goals after getting unbusy. Start allocating weekly available time for your new goals. Have your monitoring tools ready to have your dashboard up and running with the new activities. Table 13 offers an example of time ratios after getting unbusy (from Table 10) in the previous chapter.

Activities	Total Minutes Used	Total Minutes Reduced	Total New Minutes	Getting Unbusy Hours
Sleep	3,150	-	3,150.00	52.50
shower/ dress	220	-	220.00	3.67
GYM & Sports	180	-	180.00	3.00
Travel	-	-	-	-
breakfast	150	-	150.00	2.50
Eat & drink	290	-	290.00	4.83
commute to	315	-	315.00	5.25
work	2,680	-	2,680.00	44.67
commute back	325	-	325.00	5.42
Relax -family	175	-	175.00	2.92
House activities	285	-	285.00	4.75
Personal Care	165	30.00	135.00	2.25
Personal Development	195	30.00	165.00	2.75
friends & Entertainment	250	60.00	190.00	3.17
News & updates	225	120.00	105.00	1.75
Mobile - Social Media	1,100	900.00	200.00	3.33
TV & Internet	375	300.00	75.00	1.25
Total		1,440	8,640.00	144.00

TABLE 13. WEEKLY ACTIVITIES WITH REVISED, ENHANCED AND REDUCED TIME ALLOTMENTS (MINUTES)

Activities	Total Minutes Used	Total Minutes Reduced	Total New Minutes	Total New Hours
Sleep	3,150	-	3,150.00	52.50
shower/ dress	220	-	220.00	3.67
GYM & Sports	180	-	180.00	3.00
Travel	-	-	-	-
breakfast	150	-	150.00	2.50
Eat & drink	290	-	290.00	4.83
commute to	315	-	315.00	5.25
work	2,680	-	2,680.00	44.67
commute back	325	-	325.00	5.42
Relax -family	175	-	175.00	2.92
House activities	285	-	285.00	4.75
Personal Care	165	30.00	135.00	2.25
Personal Development	195	30.00	165.00	2.75
Photography				-
Write a book				-
Get an MBA				-
friends & Entertainment	250	60.00	190.00	3.17
News & updates	225	120.00	105.00	1.75
Mobile - Social Media	1,100	900.00	200.00	3.33
TV & Internet	375	300.00	75.00	1.25
Total		1,440	8,640.00	144.00

TABLE 14. WEEKLY ACTIVITIES WITH THREE NEW GOALS

Designing your pathway using the equation of success will require activity adjustments – for example, merging some activities together, moving a goal from one category to another, or decreasing or increasing other activities to better serve desired results.

Table 14 has new goals added to the goals in Table 13: photography, earning an MBA, and getting a new job. A goal of more time with family was added to other existing activities, which is reflected in time allocation, while a personal goal of losing weight was not added under that name in Table 14. It was included in other existing activities: going to the gym and/ or personal care.

For the goal of earning an MBA, we worked on it from the time available to set the goal time allocation of one three-hour class a week and study time of about five hours a week, equating to a total of eight hours per week. After a few weeks, the time ratios dashboard should reveal if we need to make any adjustments. Table 15 shows the new time ratios of success with new goals, and adjustments for existing activities to accommodate new goals.

Activities	Total Minutes Used	Total Minutes Reduced	Total New Minutes	Getting Unbusy Hours	Total New Hours	New Ratio of Success
Sleep	3,150	-	3,150.00	52.50	52.50	0.0%
shower/ dress	220	-	220.00	3.67	3.67	3.2%
GYM & Sports	180	-	180.00	**3.00**	**6.00**	**5.2%**
Travel	-	-	-	-		0.0%
breakfast	150	-	150.00	2.50	2.50	2.2%
Eat & drink - **Family Time**	290	-	290.00	4.83	4.83	**4.2%**
commute to	315	-	315.00	5.25	5.25	4.5%
work	2,680	-	2,680.00	44.67	44.67	38.7%
commute back	325	-	325.00	5.42	5.42	4.7%
Relax -family - **Family Time**	175	-	175.00	2.92	2.92	2.5%
House activities- **Family Time**	285	-	285.00	4.75	4.75	4.1%
Personal Care	165	30.00	135.00	**2.25**	**1.25**	1.1%
Personal Development	195	30.00	165.00	**2.75**	**0.75**	0.6%
Photography			960.00	16.00	16.00	13.9%
Find New Job			180.00	3.00	3.00	2.6%
Get an MBA			300.00	5.00	5.00	4.3%
friends & Entertainment	250	60.00	190.00	3.17	3.17	2.7%
News & updates	225	120.00	105.00	1.75	1.75	1.5%
Mobile - Social Media	1,100	900.00	200.00	3.33	3.33	2.9%
TV & Internet	375	300.00	75.00	1.25	1.25	1.1%
Total		1,440	10,080.00	168.00	168.00	100.0%

TABLE 15. WEEKLY ACTIVITIES WITH TIME ALLOCATIONS FOR THE THREE NEW GOALS

Table 15 offers the ratios of success for goals selected after getting unbusy. Time-wasting activities are reduced by twenty-four hours per week, with the extra available time used to achieve new, more meaningful goals. Time ratios show that sixteen hours per week, which is almost fourteen per cent of the total available one hundred fifteen and half hours per week (i.e., total weekly hours excluding sleeping time), are needed to acquire the capabilities of above-average professional photographer status. About five hours a week are dedicated to earning an MBA, which is 4.3 per cent of the total available time each week, while extending gym time to six hours per week, which consumes around 5.2 per cent of the total available time, for weight loss as part of personal care. Finding a new job requires a time allocation of three hours per week.

For a better understanding of the new time ratios in Table 15, consider the following:

- Personal care and personal development times are reduced by thirty minutes each, a total of five hours for both for the week.
- Friends and entertainment time is reduced by one hour per week.
- News and updates time is reduced by two hours per week.
- Mobile and social media time saw the biggest reduction of fifteen hours per week.
- TV and internet time is reduced by one hour and fifteen minutes per day.
- Total amount of time-wasting activities reduced by twenty-four hours per week.

- The amount of time dedicated to personal care and development is reduced by three hours, which is added to exercise and sports time.
- New goals are added, including sixteen hours a week to be a professional photographer, three hours to find a new job, and five hours a week for earning an MBA.
- The new time ratios serve you by allowing you to be healthy (exercise), have a new hobby with additional income (photography), and earn an MBA that can win you a promotion or a better job.
- Most new goals should be achieved within a year (except the MBA).

What ratios are success?

From professional and personal observations made while working with all kinds of different people and organisations in different capacities, I can say with confidence that for any activity to be considered a lifestyle, it needs to involve more than ten per cent of the available weekly time. For any goal to be achieved, it needs to involve more than five per cent of available weekly time. An expert-level achievement needs to involve more than fifteen per cent of the available weekly time, and if done for more than five years, it can mean stardom. Those ratios are not set in stone; they are flexible depending on the level of genuine effort invested and the environment you are in. They are more of a guideline, to serve as markers on your dashboard. Moving slower or faster is based on your choices.

The equation of success can be used for any goal. It can be applied in business, projects, and education, for short-, medium-, and long-term objectives. Remember, effort over time equals results. This is a framework to help anyone get what they want in life.

Do not forget to enjoy the journey and make sure you are flexible. Allocate time for emergencies and unexpected things. Life without a pathway is a random life. It is not just about where you are going; it is also about how you are going to get there. There is always doubt about the destination, but the journey is a certainty. Start with your goals, arrange your priorities, consider your lifestyle, allocate enough time, and go for it. Record, monitor, discover, adjust, and keep on going.

A journey might take a long time. It might be tough, boring, overwhelming, challenging, or interesting. Do not lose sight of your goals. It is easy to be distracted. Life happens, whether we like it or not. Things get dumped on us, and circumstances change. Life is not constant. Our responsibilities, aspirations, and conditions all change. Be flexible and prepared to allocate time for emergencies and the many unexpected demands life throws at us. It is okay to have doubts about the destination but make it count. To have more control of our journey is to break it into shorter, smaller destinations and break our goals into smaller parts with smaller tasks and smaller intervals. In the next chapter, we look at smaller projects and bigger goals.

CHAPTER 9

BIG ACHIEVEMENTS ARE MANY SMALL ACHIEVEMENTS TOGETHER

SMALL WINS, BIG VICTORY.

*"Nothing is particularly hard
if you divide it into small jobs."*

— Henry Ford

Yielding large goals requires greater efforts over a longer period. Things can go wrong in any project for any reason, and the path to success is completely impeded and achievable goals are no longer achievable. It happens to us more often than we believe. Being distracted, overwhelmed, waylaid, or the tendency to move back to our comfort zones are all normal behaviours.

We let our habits run most of our daily activities. We get hooked on managing urgent matters without thinking if they are important or not. Life happens, and we sink into our routines – we float in time – and suddenly, it is too late.

In 1992, I worked as a volunteer with Bill Clinton's first presidential campaign team in North Carolina. Winning the presidency of the United States of America is no small objective, and it was fascinating to experience firsthand the strategic planning and precise execution of events throughout the entire presidential campaign. To make it happen, the national campaign office breaks the country into state campaign offices, with each state having county campaign offices and the counties breaking themselves down into smaller campaign offices for cities and towns. The smallest-level office campaign is house to house, street to street. It is called 'grassroots' campaigning. Winning the presidency is driven by the collective winning of towns and cities, which adds up to winning counties, and then winning the state. It is a huge effort from an army of people to win the presidency, and it is done by breaking down a monumental goal into smaller tasks over time.

Having big goals makes us look good. It feels great when those goals are achieved; the sense of accomplishment is unbelievable. But in most scenarios, we give up quickly on our goals. In a study conducted by Strava.com on 800 million people, more than eighty per cent quit while trying to achieve their goals within six weeks of starting. A huge part of that eighty per cent did not make it past the first three weeks. People drop their goals quickly because the effort they are required to put in does not match their goals. In addition, most individuals set their goals without a clear pathway to success, which means no planning of how they are going to get them done. A goal is a result for a task or a project, small or large. A project is broken down into smaller intervals with clear tasks in each section. When you have completed all tasks, the project is done, and the goal is accomplished. The application of effort over time becomes clearer, more doable, and measurable as it is applied at the task level.

In addition, a delay or shift in tasks does not mean project failure unless it is consistent or completely alters the desired result, which means that time ratios are not per the plan. Success is about getting the time ratios done as per the plan. If it happens that you missed your ratios in a week, it is not the end. You can get back on track and do it the following week. This should give you more flexibility to manage and achieve those tasks every week. Success is measured one week at a time.

Perspective and planning

Working with different disciplines for so many years has influenced my way of doing things. I consider any activity with desired end results to be a project, regardless of size, nature, or type. Getting a degree, losing weight, making money, taking a trip, changing jobs, setting aside more family time, building a home, reading a book, and even baking a pie are all projects in different shapes and forms that all become easier and more doable once broken down into smaller tasks.

Our actions are driven by aversion instead of ambition

We fail because of the way we try to achieve our goals. Having a big goal is noble, even ideal. But when we do not have a clear plan on how to go about getting it done, we are easily derailed from achieving such a goal. The result is demotivating, and stressful, and will lead to anxiety, which can lead to failure. When a true failure occurs, recourse may become more difficult.

When setting goals, we think of them as a lump sum. We do not consider the devil that is in the details. We do not envision the discomfort, agonising burden, and resistance of giving up what we like. When tasks are completed, results will follow.

We slip sometimes, and things do not flow as planned. That is okay. Accept it, own it, and then get back to your ratios of success. What matters is to get the weekly tasks done. While you might fail one week, you can get back on track the following week. No one is perfect. Stuff happens. So, stick with doing the tasks one week at a time and measuring your time ratios weekly. *Before measuring your goal achievements, measure your task achievements.* Life not measured tends to be a life without achievement.

Winning is the sum of all activities that are done to win. The focus should be on individual tasks on a weekly basis. The more weeks those tasks are done, maintaining the same time ratios, the greater the success. You won't need one hundred per cent success in every task every week, but the threshold for success is to have more successful weeks than not successful weeks, which is measured by making planned time ratios for each week.

A good example I like to share is applying the approach of breaking down big projects into smaller activities that lead to achieving the project goals. This example is used in life and in business. I used it throughout my career in managing sales teams in many countries selling different things. One of the companies that I oversaw was selling accounting and tax services. Its immediate market was divided into five geographical areas, with one salesperson assigned to each area. Its customer ticket average was five hundreds US dollars per month for services rendered. For the company to be profitable, revenue of twenty five thousand US dollars or more was needed per month. As a manager, our target for the monthly revenue was forty thousand US dollars/month. To achieve this, we divided the monthly target revenue of forty thousand US dollars equally among the five salespeople, which is eight thousand US dollars per month of revenue for each salesperson. Considering the customer monthly billing average was five hunder US dollars per month, this meant that each salesperson on average had to bring in sixteen customers per month for the overall target to be achieved.

The company data showed that each salesperson visited an average of one hundred potential customers per week (four hundred potential customers per month). From those visits, about one hundred potential customers asked for additional information related to company services. Of those one hundred potential customers, about thirty asked for a proposal, with twelve customers ending up buying the services from the company. In summary:

Four hundred visits to potential customers, and from that:

One hundred requests for additional information, and from that:

Thirty requests for proposals, and from that:

Twelve signed service contracts.

In terms of ratios:

Forty per cent of proposals turn into contracts.

Thirty per cent of the requests for information turn into proposals.

Twenty-five per cent of all potential customers visited asked for additional information.

To increase the number of contracts by twenty-five per cent, the salespeople should increase the number of potential customers visited from four hundred to five hundred customers per month, focusing on the starting level of the sales process, which will trickle down to contracts signed.

Actions require three things to happen: a place to happen; a time for the action to happen; and someone to perform that action. To influence the outcome of that action, one or more of the three requirements should be influenced.

The place for an action can be negotiated, meaning that on most occasions, we can choose where a planned action should happen. That leaves the other two requirements for action to happen: time and someone to do it. The question that comes to mind is, 'Can I separate myself from my own time or are my time and I one unit?' We cannot exist without our own time; without time, we are dead. Our own time cannot exist without us. It would not be ours. This fact guarantees that the only deciding factor for any result is the quality of what we do-in-time and how many times we do it. The quality of our life depends on the quality of our actions.

A goal is reached through multiple actions. By breaking that goal into smaller actions, we know and accept the number of actions that are needed for that goal to be achieved. The greater the number of actions needed for a goal means performing such actions for longer periods of time. This is a positive correlation between time ratios and the size of the goal.

In 1981, researchers Albert Bandura and Dale Schunk worked on a study with children aged seven to ten. About half the children were asked to set a goal of completing six pages of maths problems per session for seven sessions, while the other half were asked to set a goal of completing forty-two pages of maths problems over seven sessions. What happened? The smaller subgoals (six pages per session) led to faster completion and more accurate answers than the single, large goal.

In 2007, when I was the CEO of a local conglomerate in Dubai, we acquired new businesses for the group, a manufacturer of hygiene and cleaning products for households (consumer products). The factory had been losing money for more than seven years, and my task was to bring it to profitability as soon as possible. To do so, my team and I monitored, analysed, discovered, and worked on agreed goals to bring the factory to targeted profitability as soon as possible.

Our team selected three immediate goals to work on: revenue, production cost reductions, and inventory management. We then broke down those goals into smaller ones. We broke revenues down to sales by region, then regions by customer type, then customers by size, products they purchased, and sales volumes and margins. We also broke down production costs into raw materials cost, packaging cost, waste, and rejects, and we also broke down inventory by type, turnover speed, and lead time for raw materials.

We took the challenging issues within each action and changed them, adjusted them, or eliminated them. Those changes applied to actions affected all outcomes, and this gave us healthier events. The total of those healthy events led to profitability by year-end.

Work is easier when divided into smaller, specific tasks. *Without small wins, big wins will not happen.* Smaller tasks force us to think about the details, which is the crucial part of how it will get done. Smaller tasks provide us with clarity about details. Smaller tasks are shorter milestones that reveal our progress. The smaller, the better.

During a business trip with our board of directors' team to Australia, one of the directors asked me, 'Do you consider yourself a successful person?' The question came from the most senior board member on the team, a highly seasoned professional with more than thirty-five years of global senior executive experience, who was serving on the board of more than six international companies across Latin America, Europe, and Australia. I had to pause for a few seconds before I gave him an answer. Then I said, 'It depends on what success means to you. Is it money, position, or fame? My short answer is yes. When I achieve my goals, I am successful. Every day, I achieve many small goals that take me to a bigger goal, and for that, I am successful. I am successful when my time ratios are under my control and serving my purpose.' That was not only my answer; it also was, and still is, my belief.

The difference between success and failure is the difference between doers and dreamers. The dividing line between doers and dreamers is the choice that they make on what to do-in-time. Do you control what you do-in-time or does what you do-in-time control you? The first one is for initiative-taking, proactive people, and the second one is for reactive people. *Doers make their destiny.*

CHAPTER 10

DOERS AND DREAMERS

CHOICE IS NOT A STATEMENT; IT IS AN ACTION.

"I never dreamed about success. I worked for it."

— Estée Lauder

We make plans, set goals, and start working on them with our eyes on the prize. We achieve some goals, drop some, others slip away, and life gets in the way; distractions, busy schedules, family, friends, bills, attitudes, and self-view are all interruptions. We tell ourselves it is okay. We are doing the most we can, and things will change, but they do not. If we don't change the pathway, the destination will not change.

Deep down, you believe that you have freedom of choice, and you do, but we mix up the ability to choose with making a choice. The difference is that the freedom of choice is an idea, a belief, while making a choice is the execution of that belief. A choice sets in our mind; to choose is to select and do.

Where we are today is because of the choices we made in the past. Where we are going to be tomorrow is because of the choices we make today. Every day, once we open our eyes, with every turn, at every moment, we have a choice. What we do with those choices is what counts. It is the difference.

At every moment, we are making choices. Do we choose to do the things that are part of our goals, or do we choose not to do them by doing something else, and then choose to make excuses for not doing what we planned to do? Choose to start working on your goals and complete some. Others, we forget about. Some slip away, and some completely fall off. We tell ourselves it is okay.

Well, let me say something here. The pathway to achieving your goals will always have obstacles and distractions. And, yes, I am saying it is quite simple to achieve your goals but never easy.

Where we are today in life is about what we have done with our efforts and our time in the past. Just ask yourself, 'How did I get here? What got me to this point?' Some hide behind where they grew up, but even the worst places on Earth have winners and losers. Every community in the world has its doers and complainers. All communities have the lazy, the comfortable, and the scared. The bottom line is that you are where you are because of your choices. What do you choose? To do something or not do it, to track your activities or not to track them, to monitor what you do-in-time or not, to exercise or not, to surf the internet, to watch TV, study hard, spend time with family? What do you choose? *Today's choices are tomorrow's destination.*

Several years ago, I decided that my goal was to be financially free within five years. That meant having enough income without having to work every day for it, to do what I liked to do most, which is helping others to be successful. From that point onwards, I chose all my actions to serve that goal. I reached my goal within seven years. The road to achieving my goal was hard – tough at times, and rewarding at other times. It took me two more years than originally planned, but I was not far off. Every week, I tracked my savings, investments, income, and expenses to make sure that I was heading in the right direction. I chose to work hard, save money, give up many of life's comforts, and invest the money saved, and I kept on doing that until I achieved my goal. If my choices were different, the results, for sure, would be different. Today, my choices are different. I work to influence others' lives in a positive way.

A choice without action is not a choice. It is a notion, an unexecuted decision. It is worth nothing. Goals and objectives without action are thoughts and dreams. They should be considered as lying to ourselves and/or others. With no action, we stay where we are, or worse, as life is not standing still. Things around us change. We change, grow older, and no action taken means we are falling behind. *Wasted time is a wasted life.* So often we say we are busy, but are we being productive? The quality of our lives will not change until we change the quality of what we do-in-time. We are not going to reach our goals without including them in our weekly time ratios. We will not succeed without employing the equation of success in our daily lives. A life without control will land wherever the wind takes it. Are you the captain of your life journey?

New norms

Reflect on life. Are we in control of what we do-in-time or is our time getting sucked out to the wasteland? Are our actions going to take us to a better place than where we are now?

Our brains are dealing with so much at the same time. Increased amounts of time are being sucked away from all of us. Our emotions are trying to deal with new normalities. We are trying to deal with the number of likes, reviews, followers, and stars on our social pages. Everyone on social media is competing for our attention. Innovative technologies are making our world smaller by the minute, and our horizon is becoming narrower and narrower. We are getting hooked on our devices, glued to our screens. They are guzzling our time; they are having a negative impact on our lives. The amount of time we spend on social media affects how we feel and can fuel feelings of emptiness. In many instances, accounts we follow on social media may portray a lifestyle that is not realistic as they are showing us a perfect life or appearance. This could lead us to compare ourselves to others, which inevitably undervalues our lives. We do this without thinking about it. We act like it is our free will, but is it?

Today's moments are forming your life, shaping your future, and taking you to your next destination. Are you making choices about what you do in those moments?

A life worth living

Nothing in life that is worth living for starts without a sense of clear consciousness, which leads to clear choices with proper actions. Remarkable things in life sometimes need tough choices because those choices contradict self-desire. They force us to get out of our comfort zones, resist our habits, start new habits, and give up enjoyment and go to work. They force us to embrace self-awareness and deal with the pain that arises from our truths. Most of us choose not to make those choices. We choose to put things aside. We choose not to resist. We choose comfort over pain, rest over work, and justification and excuses over self-truth. We choose self-deception, not to confront ourselves, to resist change, and we choose not *to do*.

- Do you feel that you are trapped in your job but do not have time to look for another one?
- Do you think that it is hard to get another degree while you are working?

- Do you think that saving five per cent of your current income is tough and cannot be done?
- Do you feel that you do not or cannot learn a new skill?
- Do you feel unlucky?
- Do you feel that you should be doing better but cannot?
- Do think that this is the best you can do because of your situation?
- Do you feel that no one knows you're suffering and that others do not understand?

If your answer is yes to any of the above, then examine your choices.

Decisions

We make thousands of decisions every day, small and big. Most are inconsequential; others are much more complex. We struggle with decision-making because of the way we are structured. Behind every decision, there are various psychological factors that shape the way we think and act. Some of these factors come down to cognitive bias. It is our tendency to think a certain way without realising it. While growing up, the brain sorts and arranges information in compartments. This is called self-arrangement and is how we understand the world around us. Every time we get exposed to new information, our brain scans all data compartments in the brain to see if it matches any existing data to be grouped with. Our brains struggle to put it into a new compartment as new information and new experiences. Sometimes, the brain rejects added information because no other compartment contains anything like that information. The brain sticks to what it knows instead of dealing with new and different information. It sees the alternative as a big struggle.

Without realising it, the human brain can become overly resistant to change. There are three reasons for this. The first factor is called 'status quo bias'. This is a preference for the maintenance of one's current or previous situation, or a preference to not undertake any action to change this current or previous state. The current baseline (or status quo) is taken as a reference point, and any change from that baseline is perceived as a loss. Corresponding to different alternatives, this current baseline or default option is perceived and evaluated by individuals as a positive. The second factor is 'anchoring bias', which suggests that we rely too heavily on the first thing we hear; we stick to our first impressions and tend to reject any subsequent viewpoints (first information sorted in the brain). The third factor is 'choice overload'. This happens when we are overwhelmed by the number of options that we have. We choose nothing when we have a large number of choices.

Simple steps included in this book will lead to better decision-making capabilities such as self-checking what you do before and after you decide to act. Self-checking at regular intervals (e.g., weekly) is central to the decision-making process. Watching your dashboard will take anchoring bias away.

When reviewing your dashboard, it's important to keep a check on the percentage value of your progress by grading your ratios, as you would in a school grading system, out of one hundred per cent. Above ninety per cent is excellent. Between eighty and ninety per cent is a decent job, and from seventy to eighty is an okay job. A score below seventy per cent on your Ratio of Success is less than average. To calculate your score, divide the amount of time you have performed an action over the amount of time it is supposed to be performed multiplied by one hundred per cent based on your weekly plan (actual over planned). For example, a new time ratio calls for six hours of exercise time per week. You did four hours. Divide the four hours by six hours [(4/6) *100%] to give you a score [= 66.6%]. If a time ratio calls for five hours of study per week with four hours done, the score will be eighty per cent [(4/5) *100%]. This is how to figure out performance scores every week.

When weekly ratios are descending with the passing of each week, it means that your old habits are taking over again and that you are losing control of what you do-in-time. A steady or ascending weekly score for your time ratios is a sign of success.

Keeping score is your progress control board. It will keep you on the right track, it will keep you from getting distracted, and it will keep you true to your plan, true to yourself, and true to your success.

With no score or grades, how many students would study for an exam? How do champions compete without a score?

The game of bowling is a process of rolling a ball down a wooden track to knock down the bowling pins. Each player throws the ball ten times in each game, and each time, each player gets two tries to knock all ten bowling pins down. In the first attempt, when all the pins are knocked down, it is called a 'strike'. The reward for the strike comes on the following throw. Points are doubled for pins dropped at the following throw. If nothing is dropped, zero points are recorded. The technique you use to throw the ball is up to you, so long as you do not commit a foul. Each time we throw the ball, a score is kept for all players to see. Now, imagine there are no pins to hit. Will you throw the ball at nothing? You would not. This is the same as working without a target. Throwing balls because everyone else is doing it would be a crazy thing to do, or because you are getting paid to throw the ball at nothing, which would not last long without a meaningful purpose.

Now, imagine if a curtain is placed in front of the pins so they cannot be seen; you throw the ball, and all you hear is the sound of the ball hitting the pins. You do not know how many have been hit. Is it a strike or do you have to go for a second try to hit the remaining pins? Because you are playing blind, you don't know how well you have done, and you would not play for long. Without feedback or any indication of how good your efforts are, you would be frustrated and stop playing. It is true that life is not as simple as a bowling game, but we treat it as much less than a bowling game. Knowing how well you are doing should be simple. Without tracking your time ratios, you do not know if you are hitting your target or not. Tracking your weekly ratios by recording your actions and watching your dashboard is to monitor your performance on the way to success. The dashboard is how we all continue to play this game, except that life is not a game. It is much more than that and should be treated as such.

It is a fact that when you stop tracking your daily activities, this is the day you replace truth with self-deception. It is to stop choosing and to let things be chosen for you. You give up control of your destiny. You accept floating in life without a clear destination. We tend to be what we measure. Change starts from the inside, and successful people choose to improve things under their control by applying quality effort to achieve quality results. It is the difference between doers and dreamers.

Being successful has different meanings for different people. It depends on your goals and what you want to achieve. Success must show itself; it cannot just be talk. Anyone can claim success. Being successful is your ability to answer questions about your own life achievements. In general, life has many parts. You can be successful in one or more of those parts, but is your life fulfilled and balanced? Is it rewarding? Success in life is being successful in what counts the most to you. The next chapter talks about what counts in life.

CHAPTER 11

WHAT COUNTS?

THE FIVE PARTS OF LIFE.

"Life is like a bicycle. To keep your balance,
you must keep moving."

— Albert Einstein

Where we are in life is based on our choices. Choices are not equal; some are positive, and some are negative. On occasion, we miscalculate the results of those choices. We make different choices, and only time will reveal the results of those choices. One thing is for sure. Choosing to add value to our lives is always an excellent choice. Another sure thing is that choosing to know what you do in your time is better than choosing not to know. Yes, we do not always make good choices, which is where experience comes in. It comes from the wrong choices and learning from those mistakes. It is also a way to consider the results before making a choice.

So often I have wished that I had made better choices, particularly when it comes to my career. When I first arrived in the United States during the early 1990s, as someone coming from an extremely poor family, all I wanted to do was to make money. I had an opportunity to continue my education through a program supporting immigrants, but I chose to work. I could have chosen to do both, but I chose the easier way. For sure, doing both would have placed me in a better position in life. So, I am doing more than ever with my time now – working on my second master's degree, authoring a book, running a multinational company, managing my own investments, mentoring entrepreneurs, travelling to more than forty-three countries, and spending quality time with my family. I want to do more meaningful things with my life! I want to give others the opportunity to avoid making bad choices or no choices at all.

The bottom line is we all are looking for happiness. We go about finding happiness in diverse ways through different means. I am always asking myself and others, 'What is happiness?' Is it money? Is it more time with loved ones? Is it about having a purpose, finding love or fame and power? How can you reach a state of happiness?

The daily lives of normal people are constrained by concerns of having enough money to cover daily demands, which can lead to the inability to choose. Demands are more than what twenty-four hours a day can produce. We are in a chase every single day. We cannot keep up, or even have time to think. Expenses are getting higher by the day, while income remains very much the same. We feel that choice is a luxury we cannot afford. The biggest psychological obstacle we impose on ourselves is that we must stay in the race.

In his 1946 book, *Man's Search for Meaning*, Viktor E. Frankl concluded that 'Everything can be taken from a man but one thing: the last of the human freedom – to choose one's attitude in any given set of circumstances, to choose one's own way.'

In the search for happiness, what are we searching for? Is it the materialistic things that make us happy, or things that we do that make us happy? Is it the people in our lives that make us happy, or is it our social status? Is it fame, wealth, or freedom? Happiness is not the same for all of us. Even for individuals, the concept of happiness changes from time to time. It changes as we grow older; it changes with different relationships; it changes with new possessions. Happiness is a feeling that comes from people, status, actions, and things that we do, or we have, or both, which all are temporary. Happiness depends on how all previous items affect us, how we reflect on the perceived value of such items and our feelings about them. Happiness occurs from the inside out. It is our reflection on things, a state of mind. Happiness is a choice.

The equation of happiness

In searching for happiness, we try everything we know that can make us happy or think will make us happy. We pursue happiness through money, wealth, things we buy, travelling, adventures, fun activities, working, causes, relationships, education, and sports. Anything we think that will bring us happiness, we do it, that's what we do in time.

Happiness and what we do-in-time are very much correlated. *Once we are in control of what we do-in-time, we are in control of how happy we can be.* If we want more of the things that make us happy, then our time ratios should reflect this. When we know what makes us happy but do not do it, it is safe to assume that we will not be happy. The more time we put into one activity, the less time we have for another. For instance, the more time we spend at work, the less time we have for personal development; more time for school means less time for other things. The more time we spend chasing money, the less time we have for spending with our loved ones. We chase money to buy things, go places, have fun, and have more time with loved ones. But can money guarantee happiness? The answer is no. Look at rich people; not all of them are happy, and some of them are miserable. Money comes with its own burdens and problems. *Money does not bring happiness, but it does facilitate the things that can make us happy.*

This reminds me of the famous fisherman and businessman story told within Brazilian culture. It goes like this:

A successful businessman was on vacation with his wife on the beach in a small coastal village when a small boat with just one fisherman docked. The fisherman started unloading his boat, and he had several big fish that he had caught. The businessman, curious, asked the fisherman, 'How long did it take you to catch all those fish?' The fisherman answered, 'Not long. Maybe less than two hours.'

More curious, the businessman asked, 'Why don't you stay longer and bring in much more fish, four or five times what you have right now? You should work eight hours or more. You can be rich! What do you do with all your extra time?' The businessman asked these questions, thinking, *What a waste.*

The fisherman replied, 'I fish in the morning, play with kids during the day, nap in the afternoon, spend quality time with my wife, and every evening, we stroll in the village. We meet friends, we have fun, we dance, we listen to music, and then we go home.'

The businessman spoke. 'Sure, you can do more. I am a highly successful businessman. I have an eye for good business opportunities, and I can help you to be extraordinarily rich. You should spend more hours fishing every day. With the extra money you make, you can buy more boats, hire more fishermen to work for you, and grow your business with more boats and more fishing. Eventually, you will have a big company, and you can be extraordinarily rich.'

The fisherman asked, 'How long will it take me to build that company?'

The businessman answered, 'Anywhere between ten and fifteen years. It depends on how hard you work.'

'Then what?' asked the fisherman.

The businessman smiled and said, 'This is where the beauty comes. You will sell shares of your company on the stock market and will become richer than you are now. You will be a millionaire!'

'And then what?' asked the fisherman.

The businessman answered, 'You can be free to do whatever you want with your time. You can play with your kids during the day, nap in the afternoon, spend quality time with your wife, and every evening, stroll in the village, meet friends, have fun, dance, and listen to music.'

'What do you think I am doing!' the fishermen said, laughing.

Although this is a fictional story, it holds real lessons to be learned. Things have different meanings for different people. Our views and beliefs are affected by many variables such as faith, culture, psychology, emotions, education, financial situation, parents, social structure, and other factors.

Researchers from the time of Aristotle until today continue to invest time and effort in finding out what makes people happy, identifying that the main drivers of happiness can be summed up in four items: pleasure, meaning, challenge and reward. Making money is both challenging and rewarding but not necessarily meaningful. Losing weight is challenging and rewarding. Getting a good college degree is meaningful and challenging and may be rewarding.

Coming back to the same critical question of what makes us happy, the answer to this question is not the same for everyone. Each person's answer is as unique as they are. Even for the same person, the value of things changes with time and experience. We grow older. We change and evolve, and so too do our answers to that question. It is wise to revisit the question to make sure you are investing in a future that is happy and fulfilling, however you choose to define that.

People are unique, but the same as well. All human lives are divided into five equal parts. I call them the five parts of life; they make the total life of any human. Individuality comes from how much of each part you have and/or want. Together, those five have all human life within them. Humans work diligently to fulfil those parts. How much of each part we fill is unique to us. Which part we choose to do more in time makes our lives what they are. The more balance achieved among the five parts; the more balanced life will be. Eventually, if you have an empty part, this will catch up with you.

The five parts are:

Part one: faith

One of the most important parts of human existence is faith (a belief system). The stronger the faith, the more it drives actions. Hardcore believers work on aspiration. They are fulfilled with the feeling of doing, not with the results. They believe that the results are delayed beyond one's life. The discipline, motivation, and commitment levels of a believer far exceed those of other people. Their immediate reward is getting the action done, while the final reward comes much later.

Part two: body

The human body is the container of life. Having a healthy body and maintaining healthy well-being is an essential part that gets neglected to various degrees and influenced by many things, including age, education, income, and community. When we take care of our body, our body will take care of us. Human physical life is over when the soul exits the body. We cannot do much about sickness and disease, but we can maintain a healthy body by having a healthy lifestyle, which should not take much from our time ratios, particularly if tied to other actions we do.

Part three: mind

The health of our minds is as critical as the health of our bodies. If our bodies are the containers of our lives, our minds are the drivers of that life. The mind consists of two parts that cannot be separated: one is the brain, and the second is the heart. When we think, when we feel, when we fear, when we are excited, when we fall in love, and when we hate, we use both hearts and brains. We use both together. No matter what we do or say, they cannot be separated. Put differently, can we separate our thoughts from our feelings? What we see, hear, feel, taste and smell enters our brains and our hearts. You decide what comes out of both.

Part four: relationships

Family, relatives, friends, loved ones, colleagues, and partners have a profound impact on our thoughts, feelings, choices, achievements, joy, and pain. Life without people is a lonely life with which we cannot deal. Humans are social beings. We seek to exercise our social needs, wants, and desires within our social circles regardless of how those social circles were formed. Our social circles include the most important people around us. Relationships have the greatest impact on who we are. Our parents, siblings, neighbourhoods, schoolteachers, mates, and communities are all part of us, and we function as part of them, consciously and subconsciously. We are the output of our circumstances, and our lives are the output of us, of what we do-in-time. Whom we do it with is all about our social circles.

Part five: money

While money makes the world go around, it does not put life into it. Money buys things, but it does not put happiness into them. I am not suggesting that money is not important. On the contrary, money is crucial. That is why I have included it as the fifth part of life. Nowadays, without money, life is miserable.

With money as the fifth part of life, questions that come to mind include, 'How much of my time ratio should I use trying to make money? How would I make money? What is acceptable and what is not? How should I spend it? With whom should I spend it? How does this affect my life moments?'

People in their daily activities seek to serve one or more of the five parts of life. We try to serve each one of those parts. A life with one or more of the five parts missing is an incomplete one. Life will not continue without taking care of the body that carries it. Life without the mind that leads it will not be realised; it will be lost. A life without faith, without belief in something greater than life, is a hollow life.

Life without social circles is meaningless, and without money, it is miserable. We can serve the money part of our lives by not being a servant to it but by using it as a tool, a means to do things, a vehicle to carry us through daily events. When money is not a goal but a tool, it will not consume all our time by us chasing it.

In summary, happiness is the balance we strike between the five parts of life; if one part becomes more, another one becomes less. Being elite in one part could mean reaching zero in another part.

Balance in our time ratios is not a specific formula; it is our own formula. It is what we choose, what works for us, and what we believe will get us to our goals. To be happy, our individual ratios should include all five parts of life. The amount given to each part is up to us but should not be zero.

A friend of mine graduated from college in the United States, got a job, and worked long hours every day of his professional life. Then he moved from one country to another, chasing the highest-paying jobs and saving most of his money. He was fulfilling his money goal, while his other life parts were almost zero. He did not take care of his body, or his mind. He was always under stress. His relationships were non-existent, and he hardly spent any time with his family. He wanted to be rich, have money, to be a millionaire. At forty years of age, he was a millionaire with two kids – a son, a senior in middle school, and a third-grade daughter – and because of his goal of being rich, he did not spend enough time with them. At age forty-four, he died in an accident. He died rich but with poor family relationships. I don't know if other parts of his life suffered as well. His legacy is this: a working man accumulated money to become a millionaire and died young with poor ties, and few memories with his kids. No life part should be zero, no matter how small that part is.

The Ratio of Success is not final

The numbers on our dashboards can change, and what we do-in-time can change. With achievements in life, our ratios of success can and should change when we have higher goals to reach. Ratios of success can also change when our situations change. When life changes, when faith changes, when relationships change, and when our body and mind change, our ratios change.

How can we be fully human without a balanced life, to live, love, be, become, leave, die, and have a legacy? Life is a moment. Choose how and what you do at that moment. Once it's gone, it's gone. Our success is guaranteed by genuine effort over time. Enjoy the journey for as long as it lasts. Once our time is up, it is over. Controlling what we do within our time is controlling our lives. The journey to success starts from within. It starts with a choice and then an action. Before moving to America, more than thirty years ago, my university counsellor wrote me a note as advice to take with me. I still remember that note, though I did not know the true meaning of it until years later. She wrote, *'To be chosen is wonderful, but to choose is even more wonderful.'*

If you don't plan for yourself, you will be part of someone else's plan. Choose the equation of success.

In the end, when implemented, the ideas from this book – like tracking your activities, working from the results backward, and breaking large projects into smaller ones – will have a profound impact on your life. Reflecting on my life, I am thankful for the people who influenced my path the way they did. I hope that with this book I can do the same for others.

It is never too late to choose new goals or go after existing ones. So long as you are living, you have time. When your time is over, you won't know that you are dead. Do not waste your time. Do not be like a dead person walking. Start from where you are now and move to where you would like to go. Choose your destination and go for it.

Looking back at my own journey – growing up in poverty, working hard every single day, making my first million, losing it, starting over, and making it again – I feel that I can always come back to this book to remind myself of the lack of structure within my own days before the equation of success.

No one showed me how to measure and monitor success along the way. It is easy now to look at Google Maps on my phone to know how far it is to my destination when going somewhere, which route is the best one, and the time it will take to get there. I am able to see how far I must go and for how much longer.

This book is about creating your map of how to get there, measuring how far you have come, and predicting how far you must go. It is about giving you specifics and a roadmap to succeed in achieving anything you want to achieve.

I cannot track activities and make the calculations for you. I cannot put in an honest effort for you. All I can do is show you what I have learned and how I have applied the equation of success to my life over the years.

It is up to you now. You are the decision-maker when it comes to the journey of your life.

May it be prosperous. May it be easier for you than it was for me. I hope you use it to create the life that you dream of and do all that you can do-in-time.

I am cheering you on. Do share your story with me and the rest of the world.

ACKNOWLEDGEMENTS

I am lucky to have had so many wonderful people in my life, starting with my father, a man of courage, hard work and positivity. He taught me to always do the right thing. My greatest thanks and appreciation go to:

- Ms Haya Dwani for creating a turning point in my life.
- Dr Akram Baqaeen for believing in me.
- My best friends – my kids. They make me better every day.
- Clare McIvor, Moustaf Hamway, and the rest of my publishing crew for being patient and supportive.
- And a big thanks to my team, for their support and commitment. Their support has made me the leader that I am.

I want to thank the failures, hardships, and struggles that have shaped my pathway to success.

BIO

Zed Ayesh is the CEO of one of the Middle East's largest private investment firms, the Al Dhaheri Capital Investment (ADCI) Group, and is an influential figure in the world of international business today.

With a proven record of creating and maintaining wealth for the shareholders of multibillion-dollar corporations, he has spearheaded their market entry and expansion worldwide by navigating geopolitical, cultural, governmental, and regulatory factors based on a progressive mix of credibility, transparency, expertise, and competitive excellence. His unique approach is to pay great attention to details and transformations to accelerate return on investments and seek out better ways to address market situations and create sustainable value.

He has more than thirty years of cross-sectorial and geographically diverse work experience and has mentored people from more than thirty nationalities to success. His exceptional accomplishments were the result of a dream that he nurtured when he was still climbing the managerial ladder. At that time, he dreamt of achieving financial freedom and changing the course of his life and the lives of others around him.

Backed with hard work, focus, tenacity, and talent, Zed had the option of retiring before the age of fifty. Instead, he has embarked on a rewarding journey of transforming lives and inspiring others.

Zed is now an engaging and inspiring public speaker and presenter who focuses not just on making money but on fully experiencing the beauty of life and relationships. He has written numerous pieces inspiring and guiding owners of startups, small and medium-sized enterprises, and large companies to implement proven ways to achieve long-term success while tackling the many vital aspects of life, such as parenting and education.

To date, he has built and mentored more than one hundred directors and helped establish a high-performing culture of inclusivity and respect. He is renowned for being an outstanding and dependable leader and mentor with rich local and global experiences as well as an excellent work ethic.

OFFERS/EXTRAS

Zed Ayesh is an inspirational leader with a proven record of mentoring people and creating success stories. He is available for corporate training, individual coaching sessions, seminars, and more.

For more information, please go to Zed's website: www.zedayesh.com.

For coaching sessions or speaking engagements, contact: info@zedayesh.com.

TESTIMONIALS

"Brilliant leadership book! Zed does a masterful job of highlighting the value of time, and provides practical and immediately impactful tools for leveraging time and effort to achieve your personal definition of success."

—Dr. Corrie Block,
UAE's Top Business Coach

Printed in April 2023
by Rotomail Italia S.p.A., Vignate (MI) - Italy